'The trouble we've seen...'

Women's Stories
from the North of Ireland

Silvia Calamati

English language edition published 2002
by
Beyond the Pale
BTP Publications Ltd
Unit 2.1.2 Conway Mill
5-7 Conway Street
Belfast BT13 2DE

Tel: +44 (0)28 90 438630
Fax: +44 (0)28 90 439707
E-mail: office@btpale.com
Website: http://www.btpale.com

Copyright © 2002 Silvia Calamati
The moral right of Silvia Calamati to be identified as the author of this work has been asserted by her in accordance with the Copyright, Designs and Patent Act, 1988.

All rights reserved. No part of this work may be reproduced in any form or by any means, electronic or mechanical, including photocopy, without written permission from the publisher.

British Library Cataloguing-in-Publication Data.
A catalogue record for this book is available from the British Library.

ISBN 1-900960-19-2

Printed in Dublin by Colour Books Ltd.

Contents

Introduction	1
Silvia Calamati	

Little Girls and Soldiers

1. 'Now I'll Kill You!'	13
Eileen Brennan – Crossmaglen (1998)	

Rubber and Plastic Bullets

2. Glass Eyes	17
Emma Groves – Belfast (1990)	
3. Why was that Policeman Laughing?	25
Rosaleen Walsh – Belfast (1997)	

Shoot-to-Kill

4. Truth is the First Casualty	29
Mairéad Caraher – Cullyhanna (1991)	
5. Why Not Arrest Them?	37
Ann Bradley – Belfast (1990)	

Women of Portadown

6. Writing Helps Me to Resist, Here in Garvaghy Road	41
Clare Dignam – Portadown (1998)	
7. Robert, One Night in April	47
Diane Hamill – Portadown (1998)	

Death Squads

8. 'Is John In?'	55
Annie Armstrong – Belfast (1992)	
9. With the Wardrobe and the Bed Against the Door	57
Lorraine McKenna – Belfast (1992)	

Women, Justice and Human Rights

10. I Have Received Death-Threats   60
    Rosemary Nelson – Lurgan (1998)

11. I'm a Solicitor and a Colleague of Pat Finucane   64
    Padraigín Drinan – Belfast (1996)

Castlereagh

12. Seven Days of Ill-Treatment   70
    Geraldine O'Connor – Belfast (1991)

13. 'Sign, or You'll Never See Your Mother Again'   79
    Bridget Coogan – Belfast (1991)

Prison

14. Cockroaches and Mice   84
    Martina Anderson – Derry (1988)

15. The Strip Searches   86
    Karen Quinn – Belfast (1992)

16. A Prison Within a Prison   90
    Róisín McAliskey – Coalisland (1997)

17. My Brother Bobby   94
    Bernadette Sands – Belfast (1981)

Work and Poverty

18. My Black Taxi   102
    Kathy Hughes – Belfast (1998)

19. Money is Never Enough   109
    Christine – Derry (1994)

20. My Husband Has Been Unemployed For
    Seventeen Years   112
    Marion McGilloway – Derry (1994)

Women's Organization

21. With Other Women Where the State is Absent   114
    Oonagh Marron – Belfast (1997)

SILVIA CALAMATI: Biographical Note   119

Introduction
Silvia Calamati

If I close my eyes and think about the women I have encountered over the years in Northern Ireland, the first image that takes shape in my mind is of the grey stones that serve as boundary markers separating the thousand and one plots of land scattered across Inishmore, the largest of the Aran Islands. On the map these islands show up as three tiny specks off the coast of Galway, in the Atlantic Ocean.

Inishmore presents a lunar vista, swept by the wind and pounded by the ocean breakers. The grey stones, some squared off, others jagged-edged, stand etched into the landscape on every side. There they have stood for as long as anyone can remember, perhaps since the days when the Tuatha Dé Danaan were defeated by the Milesians.

These stones have held out against the relentless passage of time and the unforgiving weather. There, by the edge of the towering cliffs, they form a protective wall around the tiny patches of land that they encircle.

Many of the women I came to know in Ireland are like those stones. They have been scarred by a war which has left the marks of suffering upon them – a suffering experienced in solitude, uncertainty and fear. And yet they are courageous, tenacious and ready to attempt the impossible in an effort to defend that which is dearer to them than anything

2 Women's Stories from the North of Ireland

else: their dignity, their families, the community of which they are a part and the right to live in a country where there will be neither war nor military occupation.

For years I had filed away the recordings of these women's voices both on tape and in my memory. For a long time I had been unable to bring myself to transcribe these tapes. Something always held me back.

Then I realised what it was. Those voices, even after all that time, forced me to re-experience the emotions I had felt the day I met each of those women. Every single one of those encounters had represented a powerful, even painful experience. Despite the fact that years had gone by, the tone of their voices as they talked and their pain-filled silences were too much for me.

Then something happened. On March 15th 1999 Rosemary Nelson, a very well-known solicitor, was killed by a bomb placed beneath her car in Lurgan, County Armagh. For some time she had received death threats. The previous year, together with thirty two other solicitors, she had signed a document denouncing the injustice of the legal system in Northern Ireland as well as the immunity enjoyed by the police and the army.

One of the other signatories was Padraigín Drinan. Today she carries on the work of Rosemary Nelson. I had met Padraigín Drinan two years before, in August 1996. During the course of our interview she told me that she, too, had received death threats.

The day Rosemary Nelson was murdered something snapped inside of me. I thought back to Padraigín Drinan and to all the women I had met over the years. I realised that the voices stored on my tapes could no longer be stifled, imprisoned within the confines of my mind and my heart. It was then that I began to transcribe them one by one. I added to the transcripts a number of other items which I had come across. A few had been handed to me as statements by

Introduction 3

women about their experiences. Others had been published, for example in *An Phoblacht/Republican News*, and later translated and published in Italy. The end result is this book.

Some of these women, like Emma Groves, Diane Hamill and Rosemary Nelson, are very well known in Ireland. Others have received no more than a line or two of print and a photograph in the papers. Such is the case of Máire Walsh: the stunned expression on the face of a fair-haired thirteen-year-old girl whose mouth had been devastated by the impact of a plastic bullet.

However, the story of many other women never got a mention either in the papers or on TV, especially outside Ireland. For instance, I myself learned of the death threats aimed at Padraigín Drinan only because she spoke at the end of a public meeting I attended in Belfast. It was quite by chance that I heard Danielle Brennan's story from her mother Eileen when I happened to be in Crossmaglen one day. The same is true of Karen Quinn. I met her mother in London in April 1992, at the Northern Ireland Human Rights Assembly.

Since the media had never made mention of them, it was as if the events involving these women had never taken place. It was this realisation that provided me with the motivation to go, literally go, and seek these women out.

In certain cases this was no easy matter. I recall that the only thing I knew about Geraldine O'Connor was her surname and the first letter of her Christian name. For all I knew, after the assassination attempt, she might not even be living in Belfast any more. Slowly, year by year and after an endless series of bus and train journeys, with the help of many, many people and a bit of Irish luck, I managed to contact every one of them.

The stories told by these women are played out against the background of the conflict which remains a permanent feature of the landscape in Northern Ireland. What they have

4 Women's Stories from the North of Ireland

in common is some agonising experience: the loss of a partner (Ann Bradley and Claire Dignam), the arrest of a son (Bridget Coogan), the death of a brother (Diane Hamill). Two of them, Lorraine McKenna and Annie Armstrong, had both survived attempts on their lives.

This book endeavours to record the way in which these traumatic events were experienced and how they affected the women's lives within the context of an already stressful atmosphere of violence.

Quite apart from the political conflict, these women are compelled to face a difficult battle. Theirs is the daily struggle with the problems caused by the widespread poverty, the chronic unemployment and the deep-seated economic and social degradation of the areas in which they live. All this is clearly revealed in the stories told by the two Derry women Christine and Marion (*Money is never enough* and *My husband has been unemployed for seventeen years*). With the exception of Rosemary Nelson and Padraigín Drinan most of these women are economically marginalised. Some of them worked until they got married (usually in temporary, poorly-paid jobs) and since then have been devoted to the full-time job of looking after the children. Just a few, like Diane Hamill, a nurse in the Royal Victoria Hospital, were able to find steady jobs. And then there are some who, like Kathy Hughes, opted for self-employment. Kathy decided to work in what was, at times, a very risky occupation: driving one of the black taxis that ply the streets of Belfast (*My black taxi*).

Nearly all the women in this book live in nationalist working-class districts. In some cases (Claire Dignam, for instance), it was the political events unfolding around them rather than a conscious decision, that drew them out of their houses.

And yet, as one realises by reading their stories, many of these women had never been involved in politics. This made them all the more vulnerable when they were subjected to the violence of which they speak.

Introduction 5

Nearly half of these stories go back to the beginning of the 1990s. Five more were collected after the cease-fire declared by the IRA (August 1994) and by the loyalist paramilitary groups (October 1994). Another five refer to the period immediately following the signing of the Good Friday Agreement (April 10th, 1998).

During the time that the bulk of these interviews were recorded, it became clear to me that the degree to which the territory of Northern Ireland had been militarised is hard to imagine for someone who has never been there. There were about three hundred army bases, of which one sixth were located in the metropolitan area of Belfast. In more than thirty years of conflict the urban landscape had been disfigured with barbed wire, iron gratings over doors and windows, watch-towers, huge police stations built next to the houses and TV cameras at every corner to monitor people's movements twenty-four hours a day.

This was the landscape in which thousands of people lived and still go on living what are apparently normal lives. In reality it was a scenario of war. Heavily-armed soldiers and policemen, their walkie-talkies constantly crackling, moved across this landscape mingling with the people in the street, their guns at the ready, aiming from the hip.

In a situation such as this it is the young children who are the most vulnerable and who run the greatest risk. All they can do is submit to what is going on around them. They cannot understand a situation which even an adult finds very difficult to live with. They suffer traumas from which they may never fully recover. This is what Eileen Brennan from Crossmaglen is telling us when she describes what happened to her three-year-old daughter Danielle after she was threatened by a British soldier (*'Now I'll kill you!'*).

From its very inception in 1921 the state of Northern Ireland was governed by means of a series of draconian 'emergency laws'. These laws grant the army and the police quite exceptional powers of arrest and search. They are

6 Women's Stories from the North of Ireland

empowered to exercise control over the civilian population and to use lethal force indiscriminately.

One of the most controversial weapons used by the security forces over the last thirty years have been the rubber and the plastic bullets. In 1973 Emma Groves, a mother of eleven children, was blinded when a rubber bullet, fired by a British soldier, hit her in the face as she was looking out of her kitchen window (*Glass eyes*).

In 1976, following the deaths of three civilians caused by rubber bullets, they were replaced by plastic bullets. With a death rate nine times greater than that of the previous type, these bullets have resulted in the deaths of fourteen people, including children and youths, and the maiming of hundreds more.

In this book Rosaleen Walsh recounts what happened to her thirteen-year-old daughter Máire who was hit in the mouth by a plastic bullet fired by a policeman one July evening in 1997 (*Why was that policeman laughing?*).

The shoot-to-kill policy was another tragic consequence of the emergency laws in Northern Ireland, an illegal and deliberate strategy whose existence has always been officially denied. Its aim was to deal with those suspected of opposing the authority of the state by killing them as an alternative to arrest.

This strategy has resulted over the years in the almost total immunity of all those involved, be they police officers or British soldiers. Scores of innocent people have been made to pay the price. Among these was Fergal Caraher, a young man of twenty killed by British soldiers as he was driving out of a car park in Cullyhanna in 1990 (*Truth is the first casualty*). Another victim was John McNeill, killed in Belfast in 1991 (*Why not arrest them?*).

The killing has not been confined to state forces. Throughout the thirty years, and continuing today, loyalists have targeted ordinary nationalists, men and women, in a

Introduction 7

campaign of terror. Annie Armstrong (*'Is John in?'*) and Lorraine McKenna (*With the wardrobe and the bed against the door*), two Belfast women, tell of the attempts by loyalist paramilitary groups to kill them.

The stories told by Diane Hamill and Claire Dignam dramatically highlight the thorny question of the Orangemen's march down Garvaghy Road in Portadown. Over the years this march has been accompanied by episodes of intolerance and sectarianism directed at the residents of the nationalist areas.

In 1998 the Parades Commission denied Orangemen the right to march down that road. Ever since then, at the beginning of July, thousands of members of the Orange Order have staged a protest outside the Drumcree church and violent clashes with the police have ensued. Today life has become very difficult indeed for nationalists in Portadown. The Garvaghy Road residents have become a community under seige. Claire Dignam tells how her writing activity helped her and many other women to find the strength somehow to go on in periods of greatest tension and violence (*Writing helps me to resist, here in Garvaghy Road*).

Diane Hamill describes the appalling circumstances of her brother's death: a young man of twenty-five, he was punched and kicked to death by a group of people in the centre of Portadown on his way home. A police jeep with four officers on board was parked just a few yards away, but they didn't intervene (*Robert, one night in April*).

In recent years several eminent human rights organisations have advanced extremely serious charges of collusion between the security forces and the loyalist paramilitary groups (see the Amnesty International report *United Kingdom. Political Killings in Northern Ireland*, February 1994).

These accusations totally debunk the stereotyped view of the Northern Ireland conflict as a 'religious war' or 'civil war' between two communities. In fact this connivance stands as

8 *Women's Stories from the North of Ireland*

proof that the British government bears a heavy burden of responsibility in this conflict. This is all the more serious when one thinks how the British government has always presented itself to the international community in the guise of an honest mediator, fully committed to the building of a lasting peace in the North of Ireland.

One cannot help but recall disturbing episodes like the death in Belfast of Pat Finucane, a prominent solicitor. In January 1989, the British MP Douglas Hogg said in parliament that he had 'to state as a fact, but with great regret, that there are in Northern Ireland a number of solicitors who are unduly sympathetic to the cause of the IRA'. Challenged by Seamus Mallon MP 'to provide specific support for what he said', Hogg refused. Mallon placed on the record that he had 'no doubt that there are lawyers walking the streets or driving on the roads of the North of Ireland who have become targets for assassins' bullets as a result of the statement that had been made' by the Minister.

Shortly afterwards Pat Finucane was murdered, in his own house and in front of his wife and children, by two gunmen who shot him fourteen times (February 1989).

Ten years later a confidential report handed to British and Irish governments alleged that members of the intelligence branches of the police and the army actively colluded with loyalist paramilitaries in Pat Finucane's death.

In August 2000 numerous documents were seized in the British Army's Headquarters in Lisburn. This event took place as part of an investigation on collusion carried out by John Stevens, of the London Metropolitan Police.

The documents revealed further disquieting details surrounding the death of Pat Finucane. His death was no more than the tip of an iceberg of collusion involving the police, the army and the loyalists.

The murder of Pat Finucane, like so many others during those years, would appear to be the work of members of loyalist paramilitary groups which had been assisted by a secret

Introduction 9

unit set up within the British army by top-ranking military authorities. This unit was called Force Research Unit (FRU).

The existence of the FRU thus reveals that the British government had for years made use of paramilitary loyalist groups in its war against the IRA. In so doing it had passed sentence of death on an unknown number of citizens of Northern Ireland.

It is against this background that the testimony of Rosemary Nelson assumes even more disquieting overtones (*I have received death threats*). One of Pat Finucane's colleagues, Rosemary Nelson had devoted her professional career to openly challenging the worst injustices of Northern Ireland's judicial system.

During the course of a speech before the International Operations and Human Rights Sub-committee of the US Congress (the text is presented in this book), Rosemary Nelson stressed the fact that a new society in Northern Ireland would be possible only when the role of lawyers was recognised and respected. Only then would they be able to carry on their work free from outside pressure and interference.

An open challenge of this nature was unacceptable in the eyes of anti-democratic forces in Britain and Northern Ireland. As I have already mentioned, on March 15th 1999 a bomb placed beneath her car cut short the life of Rosemary Nelson. As in the case of Pat Finucane a loyalist paramilitary group (the Red Hand Defenders) claimed responsibility for her death. However, the dynamics of the attack and the type of explosive used, aroused suspicion of collusion between loyalist paramilitary groups and the Northern Ireland security forces.

Today, Padraigín Drinan has the difficult and dangerous task of carrying on Rosemary Nelson's work. In her story (I'm a solicitor and a colleague of Pat Finucane) Padraigín emerges as a woman of considerable strength, who has made up her mind to stand her ground and to continue the battle for civil liberties and human rights. And yet she is a woman

10 *Women's Stories from the North of Ireland*

who is aware that the state cannot, or will not, protect her, just as in the case of Rosemary Nelson.

The stories told by Geraldine O'Connor (*Seven days of ill-treatment*) and Bridget Coogan (*Sign, or you'll never see your mother again*) were inspired by the nightmare of the interrogation centres in Northern Ireland. Amnesty International and the United Nations Commission on Torture have repeatedly demanded the closure of these centres.

The prison experiences in this book speak through the voices of three women: Martina Anderson, locked up in a crumbling English jail (*Cockroaches and Mice*), Karen Quinn, who was subjected to a brutal, forced body-search during which she was stripped naked (*The strip-searches*) and Róisín McAliskey, the daughter of Bernadette Devlin McAliskey (*A prison within a prison*). In addition, Bernadette Sands tells us who her brother was and describes the terrible ordeal that led to his death on hunger strike (*My brother Bobby*).

It is worth reminding the readers of this book that the stories related here are only a few of the multitude of voices making up the female universe of Northern Ireland. That universe is one in which many worlds co-exist. Most of the central figures in the book come from the nationalist working class. The difficulties they face are different to those of other women who share the same cultural and religious identity, but belong to the middle class. There is a class divide among women within the unionist community also. It is necessary to emphasise this since there is a tendency to portray the two communities (nationalist and unionist) as two internally homogenous groups.

However, the day-to-day lives of the women in this book are very different from the lives of the women in the unionist community. Women belonging to the unionist community have a different relation with the state, its institutions and the security forces.

Introduction 11

And yet, in Northern Ireland many women of the most diverse political and social backgrounds have come together to improve women's conditions in both communities. One of these women is Oonagh Marron, who runs the Falls Women's Centre, in Belfast. The centre works in close collaboration with similar centres located in the unionist areas (*With other women where the state is absent*).

According to Oonagh Marron women of the nationalist and unionist communities can work together towards a solution of women's problems that have so far been either ignored or given scant attention by the state.

Burning issues such as female unemployment, violence against women, abortion and health education are addressed by the Women's Support Network, linking Women's Centres located in the Belfast area with those on the outskirts.

In all these years I have met many other women in addition to those I have presented here. Some of them left indelible traces in my life.

Every one of those voices reverberated deep within me like a scream. They remind me of the painting by the Norwegian painter Edvard Munch which bears the same name (The scream, 1893). I felt I had no choice but to become a sounding-board for those voices.

This book is the debt I feel I owe each of these women for having agreed to speak of their pain with me, a stranger and a foreigner.

Their's is an intimate, deep-seated anguish which demanded of me extreme sensitivity the moment I made up my mind to write their stories down. It has been a very difficult task, but I hope I have done justice to the women's trust.

1.
Now I'll Kill You!
Eileen Brennan – Crossmaglen (1998)

Erin is the Gaelic name for Ireland. The word means 'The Land of Ériu', an ancient goddess. To some of those who saw her she appeared in the form of a huge but very beautiful woman; others saw her as a grey, long-beaked crow. She was a powerful witch who lived on a hilltop in the centre of the island. The older she became, the taller the hill grew. She would tear enormous clods of earth from the hillside and hurl them at enemy soldiers. These lumps of earth turned into fighting men and so Ériu would emerge victorious from every battle.

***

I have lived in Crossmaglen all my life. I was eighteen when I got married and I have four children. The youngest is five and the oldest is sixteen.

At the end of the seventies, when I was a little girl, life here was really tough. We didn't have that many places to go and play and there were a lot of soldiers about in that area. Even we kids could not escape their security checks and their intimidation. We were always being stopped on our way to school. They would search our school bags. We had to be on the lookout all the time when there were soldiers on the street. They even came looking for us in the youth club, the only place we could meet our friends. They would grab a couple of kids and take them outside and beat them up. I saw them

14 *Women's Stories from the North of Ireland*

do this lots of times, for no reason at all. I was lucky because I lived near the youth club, so I could go there often. But there were other parts of the town that I had no way of getting to; I would have been stopped too often by the soldiers.

Over the years the military presence has not diminished. 98% of the population in Crossmaglen is made up of nationalists. The situation is totally different to that of Belfast where it's almost impossible to tell where the boundaries between unionist and nationalist areas lie. In 1969, when the British soldiers were sent to the North of Ireland, our houses had not been attacked by the Orangemen, like in Belfast and Derry. So there was no reason for sending British troops into our streets because we were in no danger. The soldiers are not welcome here. The people never wanted them and don't want them now. The local shopkeepers have always refused to serve them.

Right after I got married, I moved to my present house and I've been living here for nearly sixteen years. For our children it hasn't been easy growing up. They have to be on the alert all the time for the army and police patrols. Speaking as a mother, I wish the soldiers would go away one day soon. I wish my children could grow up in a normal environment and not in a war-time scenario. Here they are surrounded by razor-wire, check-points, armoured personnel-carriers, watch-towers. It is an open-air prison from which there is no escape. If only they could go out of the house and go and play wherever they pleased, without being stopped, without being subjected to violence and intimidation…

The tactic adopted by the soldiers consists of staying as much as possible in close contact with the civilian population. They feel that this will function as a deterrent against attacks on them. They use us as human shields. That's why, here in Crossmaglen, permanent road-blocks have been set up close to houses and schools. They have also built a huge army base in the central square of our little town. It is horrible and out of all proportion compared to the wee little houses all around.

Having to live every day in a atmosphere of repression and violence is terrible for an adult, but it becomes unbearable for a child. In fact, the children are not capable of comprehending what is being done to them every single day. They are defenceless and they represent the subjects most at risk in a war situation.

The soldiers have no regard for our children's age. My son, Peter, plays on the local Gaelic football team. Every time he's out on the street the soldiers stop him. They ask his name, when he was born, where he's coming from and where he's going. Because of his age he would have the right to remain silent and refuse to reply, but they won't let him go until he tells them what they want to hear. The same thing happens to other young boys that I know. Sometimes an army patrol will pass a group of youngsters walking along the road and they'll start insulting them for no reason. They call them: 'Irish bastards', 'bastard fenians', things like that. It's a way of provoking them and getting them to react. The soldiers even insult the children. I clearly remember what happened to a boy of fifteen. He was dragged bodily from Crossmaglen square by four policemen because he had not answered their questions. I have seen many taken away like him.

We parents don't know what to do. Most of these cases of harassment take place when the young people are alone in the street. We only hear about it when it's too late. If we phone the police to complain, they tell us they have no record of the incidents we describe.

My daughter Danielle, the second oldest, had a traumatic experience when she was only three. One afternoon she was playing on the corner of the street with her sister Christine when, all of a sudden, a soldier appeared out of nowhere. He had decided to give her a scare and he succeeded only too well. He stood in front of her and ordered her to put their

16 Women's Stories from the North of Ireland

hands up. 'Now I'll kill you!', he said. Danielle was terrified. Christine took her home straight away. As soon as she saw me she threw her arms around my neck and, between sobs, she told me what had happened. I ran out into the street looking for that soldier, but he had disappeared.

It took a month before I realised that Danielle was starting to have problems. She wasn't able to sleep at night. She wet her bed and had frequent nightmares. She would wake up with a start and cry out: 'A soldier wants to kill me!' During the day she always stayed close to either my husband or myself. I couldn't go anywhere without her. She didn't want to leave the house and she watched TV for hours on end. When we had to go out together she always checked to make sure there were no British soldiers in the street. If a patrol came our way I had to hurry her into a shop till it passed by. Whenever she saw the soldiers she used to panic and start crying hysterically.

All this went on for about two months. I didn't know what to do, so I consulted a doctor. He said Danielle needed some help. So I had to take her to a psychotherapist. During the encounters she tried to get Danielle to talk and she made her draw a lot. Danielle kept drawing pictures of a soldier with a gun. She was able to describe his physical appearance and the colour of his uniform clearly. She recalled every detail. These twice-monthly meetings continued for nearly a year.

Now, nearly six years after the event, Danielle is still very frightened. It's the soldiers' uniforms that terrify her. She still feels the same fear of the uniforms. We have learned to recognise her reactions, so if she's out playing in the street and the soldiers enter our area, we go and fetch her into the house.

In the past she often talked about what happened to her. Not any more.

Recorded in Crossmaglen, August 1998

2.
Glass Eyes
Emma Groves – Belfast (1990)

Fithir, the youngest daughter of Tuathal, the High King of Ireland, attracted the attentions of Erc, the King of Leinster. Dairine, Fithir's sister, was still without a husband and their father would not allow his younger daughter to marry until her elder sister had been wed. And so Erc abducted Dairine and shut her up, with nine of her maid-servants, in a tower in the middle of a forest. Then he went back to Tara with the news that she was dead. Fithir, still in mourning for her sister, was now free to marry. Many years later, as she was walking in the woods, Fithir came across her beloved sister whom she had mourned for dead. The shock was so great that she fell dead on the spot. Seeing her sister lying there lifeless on the ground, Dairine, too, died of grief.

***

I have eleven children and I live in Belfast. My story began nearly twenty years ago. It was 1971, the first months of internment. At that time any family that lived in nationalist areas, with male members between the ages of 14 and 40, were liable to have their house searched two or three times a week. There were continuous arrests.

At five o'clock one morning the RUC and the British soldiers entered our street. This time they took away one of our neighbours, a young man of twenty-eight. His wife Mary was distracted. I dropped in on her to see if there was anything I could do to help: make her a cup of tea maybe or get the

18 *Women's Stories from the North of Ireland*

children dressed. While I was in her house a shout went up from the street outside: 'The paratroopers are coming!' I looked out the window and I saw them appear at the end of the street. They advanced towards us in a very aggressive manner. They were fully armed and they kept repeating that nobody was to leave their house. A soldier was stationed in front of every hall-door to make sure that none of us did.

I left Mary and hurried back home. In the meantime, the police had entered my house. They ordered me, along with my husband and our children, to stay in one room. We were literally immobilised in our own home.

I went to look out of my kitchen window. The street was deserted, except for the soldiers and the police. It was terrible to stand there watching and not to be able to do anything at all; men and boys were being dragged bodily from their homes. Some of them had only had time to pull on a pair of trousers, others were in their bare feet, still others were hauled away half-naked, manhandled and beaten. I can still remember the last one I saw, a man whose head was being repeatedly bashed against the side of an armoured car. I was shattered. I felt so helpless. I didn't know whether to cry or to start screaming, so I said to my daughter: 'For heaven's sake, let's hear a song; it'll keep our spirits up ...' She chose that lovely ballad, *Four Green Fields*.

The music had just started when a British soldier emerged from behind an armoured car. I was still at the window but I didn't see him coming because I was looking the other way. He was a few yards away from me when he took aim and fired in my direction. The rubber bullet hit me full in the face. Everything went black for me. I was carried out of the house with a towel over my face and loaded into a friend's car. But the soldiers would not let us through. They were awful moments. My daughters were absolutely frantic. They didn't know what to do. My husband had to remove the towel and show my bloody, disfigured face to the soldiers.

Glass Eyes 19

Only then would they let the car leave the area. I arrived at the hospital in such a serious condition that they had to remove both my eyes.

I've often been asked why that soldier shot me. In all these twenty years I have never been able to find an answer. You see, I didn't represent any sort of threat for those who were carrying out the arrests that August dawn.

It was a terrible experience for my family. Neither they nor my closest friends had the courage to tell me I would be blind. Mother Teresa was visiting Belfast at the time and she came to see me in hospital. It was she who told me, after taking my hands in hers, that I would never recover my sight. At that point all I wanted was to die. I was the mother of eleven children. Up till then I had led a very active life. I just couldn't accept the idea that I would never again see the faces of the people I loved most in the world or be able to take care of them as I had always done before.

After leaving the hospital I went through a long period of depression. One of my daughters had to give up her job so she could look after the house and take my place as the mother of our children. The youngest ones weren't able to comprehend such a sudden change in the woman who had always taken care of them. Without warning they found themselves having to deal with a person who was confined to her bed, unable to move. I had undergone plastic surgery and been fitted with two glass eyes. Seeing me in that state, they were almost frightened. It was quite a blow when they told me about it years afterwards.

As time went by, however, thanks to the help of my family and my friend, I managed to accept what had happened to me. Little by little I forced myself to go back to leading as normal a life as possible. Step by step I learned to walk unaided from my bedroom to the bathroom, then to the kitchen. The walls, the sharp corners of the furniture, the surfaces of the doors, all these served as my guides. Very slowly I familiarised myself with the position of the most commonly used objects in the

20 Women's Stories from the North of Ireland

house: the kettle, the fridge, the TV. I learned again how to operate the washing-machine and even the vacuum-cleaner. So I started doing some of the things I had always done before.

In 1976 the rubber bullets, of which I had been the victim, were replaced by plastic bullets. Until then they had caused the death of one person and the wounding of a further seventy. The new bullets were solid PVC cylinders, 4 inches long and 1.5 inches in diameter. Their weight was nearly 5 ounces and they were fired at up to 170 miles per hour. They were presented as a more secure and less dangerous means of crowd-control. Their use was prohibited on British soil as they were deemed 'a danger to the civilian population'. Despite this, they were used unsparingly in Northern Ireland.

In 1981, at the time of the prison struggles in Long Kesh, large numbers of people took to the streets to show their solidarity with the prisoners. The greatest number of plastic bullets was fired between May and August 1981, the very months during which Bobby Sands and the other nine prisoners died on hunger strike. During those years, the vast majority of the victims of the plastic bullets were children between the ages of ten and fifteen. In October 1976 Brian Stewart, 13 years old, was killed in Belfast by a plastic bullet. He was shot in the face by a British soldier. Again in Belfast, 12 year-old Carol Ann Kelly was fatally shot on her way home after buying milk, in May of 1981. Paul Whitters, aged 15, from Derry, died in April 1981 as the result of a bullet to the head fired by an RUC policeman. Hundreds were wounded.

It was then that I decided I had to do something to have those deadly bullets banned. In 1982 I learned that they were manufactured by an American company. So I went to the US with my daughter and an 18 year-old youth from Derry who had lost an eye and had his face disfigured. We managed to arrange a meeting in New York with the manager of the company. After our talk the company stopped producing the bullets.

As soon as I returned to Belfast I was intimidated by the police and the soldiers. After a lengthy search, my house was

Glass Eyes 21

left in a disastrous state and my daughter was arrested. Nevertheless I was determined to go on, because people were still being killed and wounded by those bullets. Most of the victims were unable to go back to leading a normal life. Broken bones, disturbed vision, epileptic seizures, permanent brain lesions: these were the most serious consequences.

The children were the most vulnerable of all. In April 1982 another little boy (Stephen McConomy, aged eleven) died as a result of shot to the head fired by a British soldier. When you start killing the children, you inflict the deepest wound of all on a country. In 1982, at the request of the government in Dublin, the European Parliament banned plastic bullets throughout the European Union. However, the British government ignored the ban.

Then came that appalling afternoon of August 12th 1982. The annual Internment March was to take place. Thousands of people converged on Falls Road. They came from the nationalist areas of Belfast and from all over Ireland. Support groups came from Britain, America and other parts of the world. There were also large numbers of reporters and journalists sent by overseas television stations. I remember it was a nice, warm, sunny day. The march went off peacefully in a kind of festive spirit. There were lots of children in the street. The air was full of the sound of the ballads played by the bands that accompanied the crowd.

When the march got to Andersonstown, the people gathered in front of the Sinn Féin offices to listen to Gerry Adams speaking. A lot of them sat down on the ground. The road was closed off at each end by the armoured vehicles of the RUC and by dozens of police officers in their battle gear. On the rooftops, behind the people, British soldiers, their rifles trained on the crowd, observed the proceedings. A TV camera fixed to a helicopter hovering low over our heads, filmed the scene. The noise from the helicopter was so deafening that we could barely make out what Gerry Adams was saying. So only a few people heard that the next speaker would be Martin Galvin.

22 Women's Stories from the North of Ireland

He was the representative of the American association NORAID and the then Secretary of State, James Prior, had denied him entry into Northern Ireland.

In the space of a few seconds, in an attempt to arrest him, the RUC officers climbed into their armoured cars, started their engines and began to move forward, ignoring the crowds of people sitting on the ground. Other policemen used brute force and batons to clear the way. They lashed out blindly at men, women and children who hadn't even been given the time to get to their feet. Photographers and reporters too were beaten and clubbed. It was then that the police began to shoot. Again and again they fired rounds of plastic bullets into the crowd. Panic broke out. Terrified, the people didn't know which way to run. Many tried to get their children to safety by taking to the side streets. The dozens of people sitting down could only flatten themselves against the ground and try to stay underneath the line of fire. Anyone who stood up would become a target.

John Downes, a young man of 22, was hit in the heart by one of those bullets. A series of three photographs taken by a reporter in those terrible instants clearly shows the policeman aiming at John's heart from a distance of less than two metres. Though he was given help straight away, Downes died very soon after, there on the asphalt of Andersontown. Twenty people were wounded that tragic afternoon, struck by plastic bullets or injured by the armoured vehicles of the RUC.

John Downes' death marked a point of no return in my life. He was the twelfth person to be slain by plastic bullets since 1976. I realised I would no longer be able to continue my protest alone. So, at the end of 1984, together with the relatives of the victims and other people who had been wounded, I founded the United Campaign Against Plastic Bullets, a non-political organisation based on humanitarian principles. Representatives of the church and human rights activists joined us. The main purpose of the United

Glass Eyes 23

Campaign was to put as much pressure as possible on the British government so they would ban plastic bullets as requested by the European Parliament.

Furthermore, it was necessary to inform public opinion of the danger of these bullets. People unfamiliar with the reality of Northern Ireland might imagine that these projectiles were about the size of regular bullets and that, being made of plastic, they were less dangerous. They could not imagine that the police make widespread and indiscriminate use of them. According to the rules, the bullets were supposed to strike a person only from the waist down after ricocheting off the ground. In reality, the high percentage of wounds to the head pointed to the fact that the soldiers and the police tended to aim directly at specific parts of the body and to fire at a distance of less than the twenty metres. As I've already said, John Downes was fatally shot by a policeman standing no more than two metres away.

Together with other members of the United Campaign I spoke of my experience at public meetings the length and breadth of Ireland. Then we decided to take our campaign abroad. We were invited to Holland, Belgium, Norway, Italy, Sweden and Germany. I myself went to the US on two occasions. Blind as I am, this was no simple matter. Nevertheless I have continued my campaign to this day.

Some time ago we found out that a Scottish factory, the Bronx Fireworks Company, was manufacturing plastic bullets. For four years a delegation from the United Campaign went over to Scotland to picket the factory gates. Two years later the factory stopped making the bullets. The are still a number of factories producing them but the British authorities keep their names secret. At the moment we are focusing our efforts on a London-based industry: Astra Holdings. We hope that, sooner or later, this company too will stop manufacturing the bullets.

24 *Women's Stories from the North of Ireland*

After John Downes, two more youths were killed by plastic bullets: Keith White, a twenty-two-year-old from Portadown (1986) and Seamus Duffy, aged fifteen, from Belfast (1989). So the death toll rose to fourteen.

Bringing those responsible to justice remains the most difficult aim to achieve. After twenty years not a single British soldier has been tried for having blinded me. I don't know the name of the soldier. It would not, however, be difficult for the British authorities to identify him, if only they had the will to do it. In all these years the only member of the security forces to be brought to trial was Nigel Hegarty, the police officer who killed John Downes. During the course of the trial evidence was presented in the form of photographs and a video showing the sequence of the killing. They were the same images that thousands of people had seen on TV that tragic August 12th 1984. And yet Hegarty was acquitted and reinstated in the ranks of the police. Shortly afterwards he was promoted.

The victims of plastic bullets are always offered large sums of money as compensation. I have always refused this money as have other family members of the victims. We do not want money. What we do want is justice».

Recorded in Belfast, August 1990

3.
Why Was that Policeman Laughing?
Rosaleen Walsh - Belfast (1997)

The Princess of Leinster, Aillinn, fell madly in love with Baile mac Buain, a prince of Ulster. The two lovers had decided to spend a night of love together in a house at Ros na Ríogh, which was midway between their two kingdoms. But an evil spirit came to Baile at the meeting-place and told him that Aillinn was dead. On hearing the news, the young prince fell dead. Then the spirit went to Aillinn and told her the same story, only this time it was the truth. Aillinn died of grief. Realising the depth of the young lovers' feelings, their people buried them side by side. Two magic trees grew from their tombs; on Aillinn's there grew an apple tree, on Baile's a yew. When they were full-grown, their branches entwined. Centuries later some Irish poets felled the two trees and with the wood they fashioned staffs on which they carved the most tragic love tales of their land.

***

I live with my family in West Belfast. A month ago my thirteen-year-old daughter, Máire, was hit in the face by a plastic bullet fired by an RUC officer.

Tension was running high that evening because of what was happening in Portadown and in the rest of Northern Ireland. The police were constantly patrolling our streets. I was afraid that something serious might happen like on the previous nights. In West Belfast that afternoon, in the space of a few hours, a march had been organised to protest against the events in Portadown. Thousands of people had taken to the streets and joined the protesters who had marched as far as the RUC police station.

26 Women's Stories from the North of Ireland

Every Sunday evening Máire went out with her friends. They used to go to a little place where they could dance and listen to music. The place, which was part-owned by my husband, was in Andersonstown Road. I didn't want to let Máire out of the house but she insisted and so I let her go. The fact that, after all, she would be with my husband served to calm my fears. The route she would follow with her friends on the way home would be the usual one: a stretch of Andersontown Road, then a brief stop at a little shop to get chips and something to drink.

At the end of the evening, when it was time to head for home, one of the two friends found that she had no company. So, along with two other young girls, Máire offered to walk part of the way home with her. A few minutes later they reached the point where they would have to leave their friend. They were in a big field a few yards from our house. By an ironic twist of fate, it was the very spot where, sixteen years before, Julie Livingstone, a young girl still wearing her school uniform, had been fatally wounded by a plastic bullet. Before saying goodnight the three girls stood there chatting for a while.

It was then that three armoured police vehicles came towards them, moving fast along the road that bordered the field. What the three girls didn't know was that a short time before there had been clashes involving the police and nationalist youths. There were still some people about. They had come out of their houses to see what was going on. Everyone ran away at the sight of the approaching armoured cars. Máire was still talking to her friends. She didn't realise what was going on, so she didn't move from where she stood. Her two friends though, took to their heels when they saw the RUC men get out of their armoured cars and aim their rifles at them. It was only at that point that Máire became aware of the danger she was in and only then did she start to run. She hadn't taken more than a couple of steps when she heard, quite distinctly, two metallic clicks behind her and the sound of someone laughing. Since she had never been in a situation like that, she thought it must be some kind of joke. Without stopping, she turned her head

Why Was That Policeman Laughing? 27

for a second to see who was laughing. It was then that a plastic bullet hit her in the face, shattering her mouth and lower jaw.

Eye-witnesses stated that the RUC officer aimed directly at Máire's head while she was running away and that she had her back to the policeman. If he had not started laughing she never would have turned round and the bullet would have hit her in the back of the head.

When she fell to the ground, her friends started screaming in horror. Máire didn't realise immediately that she had been hit. She only grasped the fact when the blood began to stream down her face. In spite of the girls' screams and with my daughter lying there on the ground, the policeman went right on laughing and firing into the air. Not one of the RUC officers came to assist her. The only one who rushed to her side was a man who lived nearby. He carried her to his house, a few yards away. Another child, a little boy of thirteen called Gary Lawlor, had already been taken to that same house earlier on. He had been hit in the back of the neck by a plastic bullet. His condition was very serious. At that moment, however, it looked as if Máire was the more serious because she was losing so much blood. An ambulance was sent for straight away.

While they were waiting, the lady of the house decided to go upstairs and get some medication for the injured little boy. It was then that the police, from outside the house, started firing plastic bullets at the front door and at the windows of the sitting-room. One of the bullets grazed the back of the woman's leg as she was hurrying up the stairs – this despite the fact that at the time there were no clashes taking place in the streets, no disorder of any kind.

The ambulance which had been summoned for Máire was unable to reach the area quickly. Over the phone, the paramedics suggested that Máire be moved out into the road so as to save time. Several minutes passed and there was still no sign of the ambulance. An acquaintance offered to take her to the hospital in his car. As he was carrying her across to the other side of the street he waved her white, blood-

28 Women's Stories from the North of Ireland

stained jacket in the air so the policemen would know what was happening. He called out to them: 'We've got an injured little girl here!' But the policemen just started laughing again and firing plastic bullets in the direction of the man who was carrying Máire in his arms. It was if they had toy guns in their hands, not real weapons capable of inflicting death.

At present, nearly two months later, Máire is still undergoing medical treatment. She lost two teeth in the accident. A third will be taken out some months from now. Only then they will be able to tell if any more need to be extracted. She could lose all the teeth in her lower jaw. At present the doctors aren't in a position to assess the extent of the damage to her gums.

Máire can't sleep at night, so she spends most of the day in bed. I don't know what she'll do when school re-starts and she has to get up early every morning. She sleeps badly and she has nightmares all the time. She's very run-down as a result of the medicines and the pain-killers she has to take. She spends most of her time watching TV. She used to be out of the house all the time. Now she never goes anywhere. She was a great swimmer and Ulster cross-country champion. She won a lot of medals. Since the accident she hasn't done any sport. It's as if something inside her has died.

In the last few weeks the police have come to our house repeatedly to take statements. When Máire sees them, she runs and hides.

I keep thinking about that policeman who shot Máire from behind. I wonder if he thought he was doing his duty at that moment. I wonder how he felt the next day and what his mates said to him. I wonder if he has children and what he told them. Máire hardly ever talks about what happened. But there is one question she keeps on asking: 'Why was that RUC man laughing when he shot me from behind?' No matter how hard I try to understand, I can't come up with an answer. I don't know what to tell her.

Recorded in Belfast, August 1997

4.
Truth is the First Casualty
Mairéad Caraher – Cullyhanna (1991)

Achtan was the daughter of an evil druid of Ireland. On the eve of the Battle of Magh Mucramha she slept with Art, the mythical King of Ireland. Art was slain in battle the next day. Some time later Achtan gave birth a son whom she called Cormac mac Art after his father. The little boy got separated from his mother and he was nursed by a she-wolf. He grew up strong and wild. Finally a hunter called Luinge Fer Tri brought him back to his mother. Reunited once more, mother and son took refuge among the inaccessible peaks of the mountains of Ireland. During their wanderings the wild animals protected them. At last they came to the dwelling-place of the High-King of Ireland: the Hill of Tara. There Cormac took his father's place and became King. His mother went to live with the hunter Luinge.

***

Between 1969 and November 1993, about 350 people were acknowledged to have been killed in Northern Ireland by members of the security forces. About half of the 350 were unarmed. Most of those killed came from the nationalist community.

A series of fatal shootings in 1982 by security forces gave rise to serious allegations of an official policy of planned killings of suspected members of armed opposition groups (shoot-to-kill).

Since 1985, Amnesty International has been calling upon the British government to establish an independent judicial enquiry to investigate disputed killings by the security forces.

In June 1988 Amnesty International published a report entitled Northern Ireland: Killings by Security Forces and

30 *Women's Stories from the North of Ireland*

'Supergrass' Trials. This stressed the fact that the laws and regulations governing the use of lethal force by the security forces were inadequate to prevent and deter unlawful killings. Furthermore, according to Amnesty International, the procedures used to investigate disputed killings were ineffective in establishing all the facts and making them public.

One of the victims of the shoot-to-kill policy was Mairéad Caraher's brother, Fergal.

***

I'm twenty years old and I live in Cullyhanna, in County Armagh. Our parents had nine of us children, three girls and six boys. My father is a farmer. My mother teaches at St. Patrick's, the village primary school.

On December 30th 1990, my brother Fergal was killed by British soldiers. He was twenty years old. Another of my brothers, Miceál, was injured in the same incident.

Fergal was working with a small firm in the area, repairing and replacing guttering. Before that he had worked in a food-processing company in Newry but had to change jobs after an accident. He had been married for two years and he had a baby boy, Brendan, who is just a little over one year old now.

Fergal followed our parents' example and he took part in many activities on behalf of our community. Before he got married, he played on the local Gaelic football team and he used to play the drum in the Cullyhanna Youth Band. All of us Carahers were members of the band at one time or another. Five of us still play and go with the band to the various concerts in our area.

A month before that tragic day, the behaviour of the British soldiers on patrol in and around Cullyhanna became even more aggressive, more hostile than usual. They started stopping us more often at the check-points and they kept us waiting longer. Some of the locals were attacked and others were insulted. Just before Christmas the situation got even worse. At the check-points quite a few people heard the

Truth is the First Casualty 31

soldiers saying that were going to 'take someone out' before their tour of duty in the North of Ireland was over. Once they stopped a car with young people on board. They made them get out and they took away their driving licenses. 'We want to have a good look at you to see if you're of bastards we're going to kill before we leave', they told them.

My father too had been stopped by the soldiers and threatened. He was told the same thing, that they were going to kill him in Cullyhanna before they left. Then one day, when he was tending the cattle in the fields, a group of soldiers belonging to some unidentified regiment came up to him. They were really aggressive and they ordered him to take off his pullover and his jacket. My father did as he was told but he refused to remove his shoes and shirt. He said that if they wanted to strip him they would have to take him to the army barracks. The soldiers replied that it would take a helicopter two hours to get to the field and take him away. However, after holding him for an hour, they let him go without calling in the helicopter.

The day my brother was killed, Fergal and Miceál had promised a friend they would go with him to Dundalk, in the Republic of Ireland, on the other side of the border. Fergal had decided to leave his car in a parking lot not far from a road block set up by the British soldiers. When Miceál arrived at the appointment he saw that two of the soldiers manning the check-point had stopped Fergal's car and were asking him some questions. When he got up to the car the conversation was over. 'Can I go now?', Fergal asked them. The soldier nodded his head and Miceál got into the driver's seat. His brother moved over into the passenger's seat.

The car started to move slowly towards the exit of the parking lot. Just as they were turning into Tullynavel Road one of the two soldiers shouted something to a third. This chap went over and joined them. Suddenly all three of them dropped to a firing position and started shooting in the direction of the car. It all happened in a couple of seconds. A

32 *Women's Stories from the North of Ireland*

burst of machine gun fire hit the car. Fergal yelled out to his brother: 'I've been hit!', and then he slumped sideways up against him. Terrified, Miceál decided not to stop and to get his brother to the hospital, but then he too was hit by the bullets. He lost consciousness and collapsed over the wheel. Eye-witnesses later declared that the car kept moving slowly forward in a series of jumps. First it seemed to stop, then it moved forward again along Tullynavel Road in the direction of Dundalk. Finally it came to a stop on the side of the road. The soldiers kept on shooting until the car went over a rise and they lost sight of it.

All they could do at the hospital was confirm that Fergal was dead. The cause of death was listed as bullet wounds to the abdomen. Though Miceál had been hit in the chest with resulting damage to the pulmonary artery, they said he would pull through.

Two of my friends brought the news of what had happened to our house. They told us that Fergal and Miceál had been injured and that perhaps Fergal was dead. My father rushed out of the house straight away and headed for the place where the incident had taken place. For him that was the start of an interminable odyssey. He had only gone a few yards when his car was stopped by British soldiers who wouldn't allow him to go any further. They told him that no one had been killed and that two men had been knocked down by a car. My father was in such a state that he wouldn't have cared if they had opened fire on him. He wanted to go to his two sons at all costs, so he insisted that they let him pass. Yet one of the soldiers told one of his mates to put a gun to my father's head: 'If he makes a move, blow his brains out', he said. A woman came out of her house to see what was going on and the soldier shoved her roughly into a shop. With the barrel of the gun pressed against the back of neck, my father thought that they didn't want any witnesses and any second now they would kill him.

Truth is the First Casualty 33

Instead, the first soldier came back, pushed the gun away from my father's head and whispered something into the other soldier's ear. Then they ordered him to turn the car round and go back. He had no choice but to do as he was told. As soon as he started the engine they stopped him again. He couldn't go on unless he gave his name and showed some ID. My father was near breaking point by this time. He retorted that they knew very well who he was, seeing as they had addressed him as 'Mr. Caraher'. But they refused to budge and made him show his ID card before they'd let him go.

He hadn't gone more than half a mile before the police and another group of British soldiers barred his way again. 'You can't go any further', he was told. They ordered him to go back the way he had come. By now desperate, my father tried to explain that, a minute earlier, other soldiers had made him change direction. Yet again it was no use: either he turned around or he would have to stay where he was because they were not going to let him proceed beyond that point. He had to obey orders. It was only after an hour that they let him go. In the end he had to make a ten-mile detour before he got to the site of the accident. However he wasn't allowed to approach the bullet-riddled car. He was able to do so only after the police arrived. Nobody said a single word about what had happened.

Meanwhile, Fergal and Miceál had already been transferred to Newry hospital. It was only when he got there that my father learned what had happened to my brothers. According to the version given by the police, Fergal and Miceál didn't stop at the check-point and so the soldiers were compelled to open fire. But my father didn't believe a word of what they told him.

The following day he had to go to Crossmaglen to make arrangements for Fergal's funeral. Once again he was stopped by the same regiment of soldiers. His car was searched and he was questioned for a long time.

34 Women's Stories from the North of Ireland

After the funeral the soldiers stationed outside our house, stopping and questioning everyone who entered or left. One of them took a photograph of my fifteen year old brother Phelim. They told him they were going to pass the photo on to the loyalist paramilitary group, the Ulster Volunteer Force. The next day a squad of about forty soldiers came into the courtyard of our house. For two and a half hours they went over every inch of it with a fine-tooth comb. Then they told us that they were now going to search our house. That was two in the afternoon. They left six hours later. In all that time they measured everything. They made notes about the layout of the beds in the bedrooms and they wanted to know where each one of us slept. They went over the ground-floor with an X-ray machine and they measured the thickness of the banisters. They made coarse remarks about the items of female underwear. They said they were searching for weapons, but they examined every single page in our books.

The harassment of our family continued during the weeks that followed. One afternoon my father was at home with my sixteen year-old brother Cathal. We had put a photograph of Fergal in the window so that it could be seen from the outside. A military patrol passed by the house. When they saw the photograph of my dead brother they started to laugh and began making insulting remarks about Fergal. So my father made a sign at them to move on and he drew the sitting-room curtains. Then he went out into the road to see if they had really gone away. Cathal followed him out. The soldiers turned back and went up to my father. 'What sort of behaviour is that? Haven't you got any consideration at all?', my father burst out. He hadn't even finished talking when one the soldiers turned towards Cathal and hit him right in the face. The next day we lodged a complaint with the police. To this day we haven't heard a word from them.

My sister Joanne, who works as a nurse in Newry, was stopped every morning for several days. Each time her car was searched and they kept her standing in the middle of the road in the cold for up to an hour. In the last few months, at different times, every member of the family has been repeatedly stopped and searched or else has had to put up with all sorts of humiliating, offensive comments about Fergal, Phelim or Cathal. We have been told that, sooner or later, the same thing is going to happen to us.

They had to remove part of Miceál's lung. He's gradually recuperating now and he never goes out alone. We want to be sure they don't keep him standing outside in the cold. It wouldn't take much for him to catch pneumonia.

Everybody knows that the version given by the police, declaring that my brothers hadn't stopped at the road block, doesn't tally with what really happened. It was made public with the sole purpose of exonerating the soldiers of all blame. It wouldn't be the first time. Eye-witnesses have in fact stated the car with the two boys on board never actually went through the check-point at all. This twisting of the facts, making Fergal responsible for his own death, is like killing him all over again.

I don't believe that any day soon they'll charge someone for what happened to my brothers. It's very hard to obtain justice in Northern Ireland. In the last few years both the army and the police have been responsible for many cases of shoot-to-kill; dozens of people, mostly civilians, have been killed in suspicious circumstances. Nothing they had done would have justified their being killed rather than arrested. And yet, since 1969, out of twenty-nine soldiers prosecuted for manslaughter only two have been convicted. One of them was given a suspended sentence. The other was freed after serving a two-year-and-three-months' sentence and then resumed service in the army.

To this day we have had no word from the police concerning Fergal's death and the wounding of Miceál. My family has continued to demand justice. The Cullyhanna community has been very, very supportive. The Cullyhanna

36 *Women's Stories from the North of Ireland*

Justice Group has been set up and is working to get at the truth. Thanks to this group, my mother and father have been able to accept an invitation to address the Congress of the United States. With the help of the Irish National Congress, we managed to organise the closing session of an international tribunal right here in Cullyhanna. Members of Amnesty International, jurists and lawyers from Britain and America, not to mention representatives from many human rights organisations, took part in the proceedings. This independent tribunal, together with the international attention it aroused, are clear signals that are being sent to the authorities of this country. All this is not going to bring Fergal back. But I hope that it just might spare other families the tremendous suffering and the hell we have had to endure these last few months.

Every time a civilian is killed in Northern Ireland there are always two versions: one given by the police and one given by the family. For a long time the police version has prevailed. Fortunately, nowadays more and more people are beginning to demand justice.

If you don't know anything about here, you must not accept as incontrovertible truth everything that is reported in the papers or on TV. Grant yourself a margin of doubt and, if you can, come and see with your own eyes what happens here. Truth is the first casualty here in Northern Ireland.

Recorded in Belfast, August 1991.

Extracts taken from Report of the public inquiry into the killing of Fergal Karaher and the wounding of his brother Miceál Karaher in Cullyhanna, Co Armagh on 30th December, published by the Irish National Congress and the Cullyhanna Justice Group, 1992.

5.
Why Not Arrest Them?
Ann Bradley – Belfast (1990)

The Irish heroine - Buan - was granted the psychic power to understand her dead husband, Meas Geaghra, the King of Leinster. When his severed head was brought to her, Buan questioned it to find out how he had died. From the way in which the skin of the dead man flushed or grew pale, she learned that her husband had been killed in an ambush. She fell prey to such desperation that she died of grief. As testimony to her faithfulness to her beloved husband, an enchanted hazel nut tree grew from her grave.

***

Among the many instances of the shoot-to-kill policy denounced by Amnesty International in the report *United Kingdom: Human Rights Concerns* (June 1991) there is the case of John McNeill, killed in Belfast in 1990.

***

My name is Ann Bradley. I run a small place called the Alhambra Café, in the centre of Belfast. I am the wife of John McNeill. I'm going to tell you how they killed my husband on January 13th 1990. He was only forty-two years old.

That morning John left the house and, like every morning, I went to work. At about one in the afternoon the phone rang. A man told me that John had been killed by soldiers in civilian clothes while he was taking part in a robbery. I was stunned, disbelieving. I wasn't even able to speak. John had never said anything to me about a robbery... The man on

38 Women's Stories from the North of Ireland

the phone said he himself was the only survivor. Then he started telling me what had happened.

That morning these three men met my husband in the street and they asked him to drive their car. John agreed. The place chosen for the robbery was the betting-shop at the corner of Whiterock Road and Falls Road. John wasn't wearing a mask and he was unarmed. When they got to the betting-shop, the three men got out of the car. John was supposed to wait in the car. Once inside, they put on their masks and pulled out their concealed weapons. They gave no sign, during the short walk from the car to the entrance to the shop, that they were going to carry out an armed robbery or to endanger human lives. Their plan, however was doomed to failure. The movements of the four of them had been tracked by the security forces. Two soldiers in civilian clothes, members of a special team, were already on the spot.

As the man on the phone went on with his story I felt as if my heart was about to burst out of my body. I wanted to scream. He seemed unable to stop and I was paralysed.

He told me that they had only been in the betting-shop for a couple of minutes when they heard the sound of gunshots coming from the outside. It was in the space of those brief seconds that John got killed. One of the soldiers went over to the car where John was sitting, whipped open the door and sprayed him with bullets. Not knowing what was going on, the other three started to rush out of the shop. As soon as the first two appeared in the doorway they ran into a hail of bullets. One of them tried to double back into the betting-shop but he didn't make it and he was shot in the back a number of times. They both rolled down the steps and onto the sidewalk. The third man, the one who was talking to me on the phone, had stayed inside. He pulled off his mask and hid by mingling with the customers of the betting shop until he was sure he could leave without getting killed.

Witnesses stated that the soldiers did not call on robbers to stop before opening fire. They also said that while the two

Why Not Arrest Them? 39

men were lying dead there on the sidewalk, the soldiers re-loaded their sub-machine guns and fired more rounds into the lifeless bodies, to make sure they had killed them.

In the North of Ireland you don't have the right to be informed of the death of a family member if he or she has been killed by the security forces. Only today, eight months later, have I received the first official document informing me of John's death. The document, however, confines itself to the results of the autopsy. To this day neither the police nor the military authorities have communicated with me.

So only now I have learned how John was killed. They fired a burst of six bullets into him. The one that actually killed him was fired from a distance of less than twenty inches. I had always thought he had died after the first bullet. Six bullets… Only takes one to kill a man…

Eye-witnesses reported that John had made no suspicious movements. But then why did the soldier not tell him to 'freeze' before they opened fire? And why did he go on shooting after John was already dead? They could have arrested them all instead of gunning them down. Now John would be in Crumlin Road prison and not in Milltown cemetery.

These thoughts keep boring into my mind. I will end up going mad.

In any democratic country of the world the law says you can not take the life of a person who is merely suspected of having committed a crime. But here, in Northern Ireland, in thirty years of war dozens of people have been killed by the security forces. I remember clearly what happened to Aidan McAnespie. On his way to play Gaelic football, this young man was fatally wounded by a bullet fired by a soldier at the Aughnacloy checkpoint. And like him, many others lost their lives.

Today all I hope for is that those responsible for the death of John and the other two men will be brought to court and tried. Everything is now in the hands of the Director of Public Prosecutions, whose responsibility it is to decide whether the

40　*Women's Stories from the North of Ireland*

person who carried out these three murders ought to be tried. I can't bear to think that this will not happen.

In the Crumlin Road prison there are thirty-four people awaiting trial for the killing of a policeman in 1988. What kind of justice is this, when a crime suspect is treated differently depending on whether he is a member of the police or a civilian?

Since John was killed I have tried to lead a normal life. I spend nearly the whole day working in my café. There's a lot to do in the mornings, but after three in the afternoon fewer people come in. I stay in the back preparing the food and I wait on the tables. Two other women work with me. My daughter often comes to lend a hand too.

After John's death I moved to another part of West Belfast. I couldn't face up to living in what had been 'our' house. After that terrible January afternoon, I never went back there. I sent my daughter to pick up my things. I couldn't bring myself even to cross the threshold.

When I find myself alone I do my best not to think about what happened, but I find it very hard. There's one thought that never leaves my mind. The same image is always there before my eyes: the soldier approaches the car, he opens the door and starts shooting. One after the other the bullets hit John in the head, in the arm, in the eye from a distance of less than half a metre…

I keep asking myself what went through John's mind in the few moments it took for him to die. I do hope he didn't realize anything.

Recorded in Belfast, August 1990

In December 1990 a ruling by the Director of Public Prosecutions stated that no member of the security forces would be tried for the death of John McNeill and the other two men. Case closed.

6.
Writing Helps Me to Resist, Here in Garvaghy Road
Clare Dignam – Portadown (1998)

Bóinn was the goddess of the river Boyne. The legend says that one day Bóinn decided to go to the forbidden well of Sídh Nechtan, at the source of the river. The well belonged to her husband, the god Nechtan, and no one could go near to it. Nine magic hazel nut trees grew there, carrying the the fruits of knowledge. The fruits would fall into the well and would be eaten by a small salmon, the wisest creature in the world. As soon as Bóinn reached the forbidden well the waters rushed out of the depths of the earth, turned into an impetuous torrent and swept her away. Yet, as the waters could not recede into the bowels of the earth, they flew down the slopes of the Irish mountains, bringing spiritual richness to mankind.

***

I'm a woman from Portadown. I live in Garvaghy Road and I've got four children. Garvaghy Road is one of the few nationalist areas in Portadown. It is a poverty-stricken area. Even though it winds along for nearly two miles, there are just one chemist's, one phone-box and three little shops.

Garvaghy Road is also the road along which the Orange Order marches on the first Sunday in July to commemorate the Battle of the Boyne (1690), when William of Orange, the Protestant King, defeated the Catholic King James II. They have always marched along our road, even though it's not the only route leading from the Protestant church of Drumcree to the centre of the city. They say they have always done this and so they have the right to.

42 Women's Stories from the North of Ireland

In recent times, their parades have been accompanied, for days on end, by very serious episodes of violence and intimidation directed at the houses and the property of the nationalists. That's why there has been considerable opposition to having these marches coming through our street. We don't ask for the parade to be banned but only for it to be re-routed so as to bypass the nationalist areas.

At the beginning of the nineties some people in my area started to get organised. Then more and more people came out of their houses to take part in the protests. It became clear that we needed a group that could speak for all the residents. And so the Garvaghy Road Residents' Coalition was born.

In July 1996 heavily armed police, in full riot gear, came in their hundreds to violently clear Garvaghy Road of a sit-down protest, using batons, boots and plastic bullets. Many people were injured, including women and youths. In July 1997 we residents were convinced by the authorities that the Orangemen would not be allowed to march through our estate. Yet nothing could have been further from the truth; the police and the army turned our road into a prison for twelve hours. Over one thousand police officers, with more military personnel, were sent to Garvaghy Road. Some eighty men, women and youths took part in a sit-down protest. They linked arms in a desperate bid to prevent the police taking control. Then the RUC started the 'road-cleaning' operation. Sixteen people were injured and there were countless bloody heads.

This year (1998) the Commission set up to regulate the summer parades denied the marchers access to Garvaghy Road. Day after day thousands of Orangemen gathered in front of the Drumcree church. They threw stones and petrol bombs in a stand-off with two thousand soldiers and RUC policemen. A trench was dug near the church to keep the protesters confined. In the centre of Portadown some nationalists were driven out of shops just like the Jews in the days of the Nazis. In the rest of Northern Ireland more than a hundred houses in Nationalist areas were attacked and ten

Writing Helps Me to Resist, Here in Garvaghy Road 43

Catholic churches were set on fire. But the most tragic event was the deaths of Jason, Mark and Richard Quinn, three brothers who were seven, nine and ten years old respectively. They were burnt alive as they slept in their beds when an incendiary bomb was thrown at their house in Ballymoney.

Even today the situation is very tense here in Garvaghy Road. Every evening, since the beginning of July, scores of Orangemen stand for hours at the end of the road. Even though these gatherings are illegal, the police who are stationed there in their armoured cars refuse to intervene. The Orangemen yell insults, throw stones and petrol bombs in the direction of our houses and only leave late at night. Ours is a community under siege.

I got married very young, just after I left school. I was only eighteen at the time. Then the babies came. I worked for about three years but then I had to give up my job because I had nobody to look after the kids while I was out of the house.

Just over a year ago my husband died. I found myself all alone with four children to bring up. My husband's death opened up an abyss inside of me. For a long time I just drifted along aimlessly in the grip of desperation and my own loneliness. Then I realised that I had to do something for myself or I'd go mad. Besides, my day-to day-obligations towards the children kept me from letting myself go altogether. Somehow or other I had to react.

So I decided to do voluntary work one evening a week at the community centre in Garvaghy Road, working with the young adolescents of my community. This is a prevention project aimed at light drugs, whose use has become more and more widespread in recent years. The project is the result of the self-organized activities of our people: we don't get a penny from the state. We organise group activities. One evening a week, under our supervision, the kids can come and watch TV, play cards or board games. Some of them are very fond of us. I have also joined a group open to women with small children. We meet at the community centre and

44 Women's Stories from the North of Ireland

we discuss our problems. These meetings get me out of the house and away from the housework at least once a week, when the children are at school.

But what has helped me more than anything else has been my experience with the other women in the creative writing group. This group was set up as part of the numerous projects carried out by the community centre. Once again, the idea was to encourage women to get out of the house and take part in activities that interested them. For years I had been writing as a way of expressing myself. Of an evening, after putting the kids to bed, I always used to sit down and write something. I wasn't keeping a diary. I'd just write down what I was feeling. For me it was like having someone to talk to, because once the children were in bed I had nobody there with me. All I had to keep me company was the housework I still had to do, the television, a cup of tea and my cigarettes. But also boredom, loneliness and depression. Writing really did help me a lot.

The teacher who runs the group explained the meaning of creative writing. I don't know if what I mean by creative writing is really that. For me it's just being able to write down the thoughts that cross my mind. Often I'm still awake in the wee hours of the morning. So I get up and start writing. What comes out is the pain I feel over the loss of my husband and, inevitably, the tense situation that we have to live with here in Garvaghy Road.

One day I showed the group the stuff I had written years before. I realised then the quality of my writing compared to now. I told them how it hadn't always been easy for me to put down my feelings on paper. When we write we reveal ourselves. Writing becomes the mirror of our souls. It means sending ourselves a letter and having the courage to read what it says. It allows us to become more aware of what we really are.

The same thing happens to the other women in the group. For some of them it is even harder than for me. They're in

Writing Helps Me to Resist, Here in Garvaghy Road 45

their fifties and they've never written anything since the day they left school. Very often they too are still awake at three or four in the morning, when they can't get to sleep on account of what goes on every night in Garvaghy Road. For all of us writing becomes a painful experience. It is a mentally and emotionally difficult task. However, no one of us has dropped out of the group. Writing is a great help to us. It helps us to resist.

Every time we met we would end up talking about what was happening every day in Garvaghy Road. This was inevitable, considering how serious the situation was. We wondered what the Orangemen would do, how the police would react, how we ought to behave. But one day, at our teacher's suggestion, we decided to stop just talking about these things and instead go home and write down what we felt. We could express our thoughts in poetry or prose. The tone could be sad or ironic, depending how we felt. So that's what we did. Every week we brought something new to read out to the others. Slowly we began to realise how deeply the events at Drumcree were affecting our lives. In fact, most of what we wrote wasn't about our personal or private lives but about what had happened in Garvaghy Road, especially in July 1996 and 1997.

One day we had an idea. We would collect our feelings in a book. At first we used to joke about it because we thought we would never be able to write a book about the women of Garvaghy Road. Bit by bit though, we started to believe we could do it. This year (1998) we have managed to print a thousand copies of a little book entitled Garvaghy Road Women Writers. It's a collection of poems, thoughts and feelings that have to do with what we have gone through and witnessed over the last three years. It's not just 'our' book. It has become the voice of our whole community. The book is an important step. Our objective is to bring it home to the people who don't live here how profoundly this situation is affecting the everyday life of each one of us.

46 Women's Stories from the North of Ireland

Last April I started to write a short story. It's about a Catholic family with three children, two girls and a boy. The boy is an adolescent who wants to respond to Orange violence with more violence. The mother is a very strong woman. The father has a good job. His employers are unionists and he doesn't want to have anything to do with the events going on around him. One of the girls' teachers doesn't agree with the position of the Garvaghy Road residents. He wants the Orangemen to be allowed to march along the road. He himself doesn't live there so he doesn't know what it's like to live under siege.

I spoke to some of the youngsters in my drugs-prevention programme about this story. They were really enthusiastic. When it's finished, we're going to turn it into a play for the theatre.

Recorded in Portadown, August 1998

7.
Robert, One Night in April
Diane Hamill – Portadown (1998)

The Irish harp was invented by one of the most ancient goddesses of Erin, Canola. According to the legend, one day Canola quarreled with her lover and abandoned his bed to walk the night. All of a sudden she heard the sound of beautiful music and she paused to listen. Very soon she fell asleep out there in the open air. When she woke up, she realised that the music had been created by the wind as it blew through the decayed tendons still attached to the skeleton of a whale. Seeing this and recalling the sweetness of the melody she had heard, Canola fashioned the very first Irish harp.

***

Diane is the sister of Robert Hamill, a young man who was punched and kicked to death by a group of loyalists in the spring of 1997. A jeep with four police on board was parked nearby and yet not one of them intervened to prevent this murder.

***

I'm twenty-nine. I'm a nurse. I work at the Royal Victoria Hospital in Belfast, but I live in Portadown, in a street not far away from Garvaghy Road.

There are ten children in my family: five boys and five girls. My father is a gardener. My mother stays at home and looks after the youngest ones. I'm the second-born and the oldest of the girls. The fourth child was Robert. He was twenty-five when he was killed.

48 Women's Stories from the North of Ireland

The town I live in has a population which is 85% unionist. There is very strong backing for the loyalist paramilitary group, the Loyalist Volunteer Force. For the thousand-odd nationalists who live there, Portadown today is a very dangerous place. In the past you risked being insulted or attacked. Now you can get killed. Things get really tough in the summer, during the Orangemen's marching season. On the night before the 12th of July they gather around a bonfire a few yards away from us. They throw petrol bombs and stones at our houses and they yell insults at us.

Our area is poor and deprived. There are no facilities for children and adolescents. All they have is the youth club that's open four evenings a week for two or three hours. In Portadown nationalists have no place where they can meet and socialize. Apart from a couple of pubs, there's nowhere else to go. When I was a teenager, I had to go to some other town nearby, like Lurgan, Newry or Armagh, if I wanted to meet my friends. All public places in the centre of Portadown were too dangerous for us.

Like lots of other nationalists, I too have to take precautions whenever I move around, especially at night. For instance, to enter our area, you have to go down one street and then turn left. When I come home by car I never switch on the indicator too soon. I leave it till the last minute so that if there's anyone behind me or on the footpath, they won't know where I'm heading. Sometimes I don't use the indicator at all. Often, if I'm driving with one of my little brothers sitting next to me, I cover his face with my hand so he won't be recognised. This is very hard to do with my youngest brother who's only fourteen. I always tell him to cover his face but he doesn't always listen. He never goes too far from the house on his own. He goes to the shopping centre and then back home right away. One time he used to go as far as the library and the shops in the centre of town. He doesn't do it any more now. It's too risky. Every now and then, when I have the time, I offer to go with him. However,

Robert, One Night in April 49

it's not all that easy for me either. After what happened to Robert I hear people shouting abuse at me in the street.

As a result of this situation, two of my brothers have gone away to live in England. The first one left a couple of years ago because, like a lot of other nationalists, he wasn't able to find a job here. The other couldn't face living here after what happened to Robert. I, too, was forced to leave Portadown and look for work elsewhere. After taking my diploma in nursing in 1991, I moved to London and I worked there till 1996. I was quite happy in my place of work. There were lots of Irish girls doing the same job. But I didn't like London. It was too big, too chaotic. And then things aren't easy for the Irish who live in England. There's still a lot of racism. Some of the girls I got to know had the question of their birthplace thrown in their teeth. Other Irish fellows found themselves being addressed as 'Paddy'.

I missed my family too much in London, so I decided to go back to Ireland. After returning, I worked in two nursing homes. Then I was taken on at the Belfast Royal Victoria Hospital in August 1997, three months after Robert's death.

My brother was crazy about sport. He played on the local Gaelic football team and he attended the weekly training sessions. He enjoyed going to the greyhound racing with my father and he used to tell us stories about what went on during the races. He got a kick out of telling us all those anecdotes. He was very close to our parents and since he was the tallest in the family, he was very protective towards us girls. He was a good-looking young man, very outgoing and cheerful. He was working as a bricklayer along with my older brother. He had two children, one five years old and the other four. He was about to get married when they killed him. His partner was six months pregnant with their third child, a girl.

After the babies came, Robert's whole life centered around them. He tried to work as much as he could so as to be able to provide them with a decent standard of living. He spent all his free time with the kids and he only saw his friends every

50 Women's Stories from the North of Ireland

now and then. He never had anything to do with the police or the soldiers. He had no interest in politics and he was never subjected to any sort of intimidation or ill-treatment by either the police or the army.

That night he just happened to be in wrong place at the wrong time. At one in the morning of April 27th 1997 Robert was on his way home with our cousins Joanne and Siobhan and Siobhan's husband, Gregory. They had spent that Saturday evening at St. Patrick's Hall, which belongs to the Catholic church, right in the centre of Portadown. They had tried to call a taxi but there were none free. So they decided to go home on foot. It was less than a quarter of an hour's walk. The only dangerous point along the way was where the road meets Market Street, the main street of Portadown. However, they would be safe once they got to Woodhouse Street.

As they were walking along Thomas Street, they spotted a group of people standing at the crossroads. They knew that they must be loyalists; no nationalist would ever have dared to hang about in the town centre at that time of night. They debated about the best thing to do. They weren't really sure it was safe to go that way, not knowing whether the other group would stay where it was or move on. The fact that a police jeep was parked close to Woodhouse Street reassured them. Surely nothing could happen with the police just a couple of yards away. So they decided to walk on as far as the crossroads. When they got there, however, they discovered that the group was much bigger than they had imagined when they had seen it in the distance. There were about thirty people, men and women.

By that time it was too late. There was no escape for Robert and the others. As soon as the group saw the five of them, they started to move in their direction. They knew that they were nationalists. They had seen them going towards Woodhouse Street and they guessed they were coming from St. Patrick's Hall. They surrounded them, separated Robert and Gregory from the girls and then they started punching

Robert, One Night in April 51

them. The two boys fell to the ground. Unlike Gregory, Robert lost consciousness immediately; after he hit the ground he did not even raise his arms to try and protect his head from the blows. The first kick to his head came as he lay there on the sidewalk. More kicks followed and others again. This went on for several minutes.

My two cousins, terrified out of their wits, could only stand helplessly by, unable to stop what was happening. One of them managed to break loose and she ran towards the police jeep, a few yards away. But the RUC people inside kept observing the scene without intervening or calling for back-up. Hearing the shouts for help, some of the customers rushed out of a pub in Woodhouse Street and tried to reach Robert and Gregory. They didn't make it because the group blocked the roadway and started attacking them, driving them back. At this point one of the men from the pub ran to the jeep. He literally hauled one of the policemen bodily out of the jeep and begged him to do something. But the officer just stood there, watching impassibly. Soon after, he climbed back into the jeep.

Meanwhile the loyalists, realising the seriousness of Robert's condition, stopped their kicking and stood around him in a circle, staring down at him. In their desperation my two cousins flung themselves on the two inert bodies on the ground. The four policemen didn't move even then. They got out of their jeep only when the ambulance arrived. Robert lay with his chin on his chest. He had stopped breathing but the officers never approached him at any time. He was rushed to hospital along with Gregory, who had also lost consciousness.

That night I was working in a nursing home at Carnlough on the Antrim coast, sixty miles from Portadown. It's a beautiful seaside place and my mother had decided to come and visit me for the weekend. My aunt phoned her in the middle of the night to tell her that Robert had been attacked by a group of thirty people. Out of her mind with worry, she rushed to give me the news in the early hours of the morning. We drove as fast as we could to the Royal Victoria Hospital in Belfast where

52 *Women's Stories from the North of Ireland*

they had taken Robert. We found him in intensive care. His skull was broken and he had a long gash on the left side of his head. At first no abnormality showed up on the brain scan. We thought then Robert was going to make it. But the damage caused to his brain was so widespread that it could not be detected even by the hospital's sophisticated equipment.

Gregory emerged from a coma and, very slowly, he managed to recover after a lengthy convalescence. Nothing could be done for Robert. After twelve agonizing days, he died on May 8th, 1997.

The last time I saw him I didn't know that he would soon be dead. The doctors told us that he had survived the most critical phase. Now we could only wait for him to slowly regain consciousness a little at a time. Only then would we know if he would go back to being a normal human being or if he had suffered irreversible brain damage. That afternoon I went to see him with my mother and my sister. When the doctor told us that Robert had just died, it was as if the sky had fallen in on us.

The Monday after the attack on Robert I consulted a solicitor, with a view to bringing charges against the police for not intervening. He was of no help at all, so the family decided to contact Rosemary Nelson, a brave lawyer from Lurgan. We sued the police. We also demanded that the four officers involved in the incident be suspended and that the government set up an independent enquiry into what had happened.

The day after the incident, the police issued a statement claiming that it had been a clash between rival factions. They distorted all the facts so as to give the impression that Robert had got himself involved in a street brawl. Ten days after, the police changed their version of the facts and issued another statement in which they made reference to an 'unprovoked attack'. Only when Robert was already dead did the RUC finally admit that it had been 'sectarian aggression'.

They waited thirteen days before arresting someone. Of the six people charged with Robert's murder, five were released

Robert, One Night in April 53

after six months because there was no longer anyone willing to testify against them. As for my cousins and Gregory, they were not in a position to identify any members of the group. Today there is only one person still in prison, awaiting trial for Robert's death. His name is Mark Hobson. The single piece of evidence against him is a statement made by a policeman. This officer confined himself to saying that he had seen Hobson standing over Robert as he lay on the ground. He had seen Hobson raise his foot as if in the act of kicking. He added, however, that he had been unable to observe the completion of this action and that therefore he could not tell if Hobson had actually kicked Robert in the head. In all probability Hobson will walk free as there is no proof of his guilt. (Hobson was indeed freed after this interview took place.)

To this day no independent enquiry into Robert's death has been set up. Furthermore, not one of the four RUC policemen has so far been suspended from service. My family has started collecting funds to finance a private enquiry. Our investigation of the facts will be entrusted to an eminent English lawyer but it's going to take lots and lots of money.

I have now become the spokesperson for our family. Most of my free time is taken up with maintaining contact with our solicitor and participating in public meetings where I speak of what happened to Robert. I was also invited to London where I offered my own testimony within the framework of a campaign in favour of Stephen Lawrence. Stephen is the young black boy who was killed, in the same manner as my brother, by a group of right-wing youths.

I'm often asked how I feel when I think about those four police officers who didn't lift a finger to help my brother, condemning him to an atrocious death. Obviously, I cannot come to terms with his death. And yet, at the same time, I can't say that something of that nature was unthinkable in Portadown. In our town there are those who look on us nationalists as second-class citizens. To others we are inferior beings. They consider us to be something less than human;

54 *Women's Stories from the North of Ireland*

in order to be able to kill someone by kicking him in the head, with the odds thirty to one in your favour, you've got to be able to strip him of his humanity. How would you otherwise find the stomach to do something like that?

Recorded in Belfast, August 1998

8.
Is John In?
Annie Armstrong–Belfast (1992)

Airmeith was one of the most ancient goddesses of Ireland. Together with her father, Dian Céacht, Airmeith stood guard over the Fountain of Eternal Youth. She had the power not only to heal the wounds of the Tuatha Dé Danann but even to bring the dead back to life. Airmeith was well versed in the use of medicinal plants; a gift she had acquired on the death of her brother Miach. Miach had been murdered by Dian Céacht, his own father, because he was jealous of his son's knowledge. Airmeith organised a magnificent funeral ceremony in honour of Miach. A host of plants and herbs and flowers sprang from his tomb. Airmeith spread them out on her cloak, arranging them according to their medicinal virtues. But Dian Céacht mixed them all up together and so now no one knows what healing powers they possess.

***

It was nine o'clock at night. I had just come home after taking part in a City Council meeting. My eldest boy was in his room upstairs. I was in the sitting-room below with my other two children, watching TV. After a bit, one of them left the room to go to the bathroom. So there was just the two of us left downstairs: my eldest daughter Frances and myself. She was sitting on the floor, right in front of the TV screen.

A couple of seconds later a car stopped in front of the house. We heard the door open and shut. Frances pushed the curtain aside a fraction and peeped out. 'Mum! A man has just run into our garden. He's got his face covered!' I instinctively got up and went to the intercom. As a precaution, I had got them to install it in the sitting-room. Putting it next to front

56 Women's Stories from the North of Ireland

door would have been too dangerous. Frances got up too and ran to my side. That's what saved our lives.

I asked who it was at the door. A young man's voice asked me if John was in. I didn't have time to tell them that no one of that name lived with us before the shooting began. My daughter and I threw ourselves on the floor. We clung to one another with the bullets coming from all angles. I could hear my two sons screaming in terror upstairs. I shouted as loud as I could to let them know we were still alive, but the noise of the firing was so loud that it drowned out every sound. Frances was screaming too.

Thirteen bullets reached the room where we were. One of them hit the TV screen, in front of which Frances had been sitting until a few seconds before. The gunfire had been directed towards the sitting-room, so as to hit anyone who happened to be there at that moment. And yet, you couldn't see into the room on account of the heavy window curtains. The rooms in my house are arranged differently to the rooms in the other houses in our street. How did they know that it was the sitting-room they were shooting at? The only people who could possibly have known were the police. They had carried out many searches in our house.

When the shooting stopped I heard again the sound of a car door opening and shutting quickly. They had to turn the car around before they could leave. My house is in a cul-de-sac in the centre of Twinbrook.

The police were informed, a few seconds after the firing stopped, of the colour, the make and the registration number of the car; two boys who happened to be in the street at the time had managed to take down all the information needed to identify the car. In spite of this, nobody stopped that car. It succeeded in covering seven miles without being spotted and stopped by any of the many soldiers and policemen who patrol every street in our area day and night. All the RUC found was the registration plates, discarded in a unionist neighbourhood.

Recorded in Belfast, August 1993

9.
With the Wardrobe and the Bed Against the Door
Lorraine McKenna – Belfast (1992)

The lovely goddess and Queen of Ulster, Macha, lived with a mortal King, Neimheadh. While she was pregnant, the King boasted that she could run more swiftly than any horse. So he forced her to take part in a race which the goddess, though heavy with child, won easily. But she had no sooner crossed the finishing line than she gave birth to twins and died, laying a curse on all the people of her husband's tribe. As a result of 'Macha's curse' when any man of Ulster was in danger he would be seized with labour pains lasting five days and four nights. One man alone, Cú Chulainn, was immune from this curse.

***

I live in Springfield Park, West Belfast, with my husband Gerard and our two little girls: Debbie, aged six, and Christina, aged four.

It was about one in the morning. The babies were asleep in the room next to ours. My husband was woken up suddenly by a banging on the front door. He realised the danger at once. At that time loyalist groups had broken into the homes of lots of families in our road, intent on killing the occupants. Terrified, Gerard shook me awake. Then, as fast as he could, he began shoving the wardrobe up against the bedroom door to form a makeshift barricade. I panicked. He yelled at me to help him push the bed too, to block the entrance better.

In those few seconds I managed to glance out of the window. I saw two armed men breaking down our front

58   Women's Stories from the North of Ireland

door. The sound of the blows echoed in the silent street. Then we heard their footsteps on the stairs, coming closer and closer. Gerard tried frantically to push the bed as hard as he could against the wardrobe. It was then that we heard them go into the babies' room. I completely lost my head. I started screaming and I grabbed the end of the bed, trying to pull it away from the wardrobe. I wanted to rush out of the room and save my babies. My husband had to throw me to the floor and hold me down with all his strength. Then the shooting started. A stream of bullets ploughed through the door, raking every corner of the bedroom. For a long time they repeatedly tried to break down the door and get in, but they weren't able to. At last they decided to leave. We heard their footsteps going down the stairs, then nothing more.

A deathly silence enveloped us. Still stretched out on the floor, Gerard and I were paralysed with fear. Our minds were filled with anguish over the fate of our children. It was a long time before we mustered the strength to stand up. We moved the furniture away from the door and ran to the children's room. They were very frightened but they were safe and sound. My husband ran to phone the police.

Like an automaton I rushed out of the house. I ran to Brenda Murphy's house. Yelling at the top of my voice, I hammered on her front door. Brenda was in the house with a neighbour, Lorraine Halpenny. Sobbing and distraught, I told them how a group of people had tried to kill my family and me. Brenda said she had heard the shooting and that she had already called the police. Out of my mind with fear, I begged the two women to do something. Brenda rushed to my house. She went upstairs, where the air made breathing difficult. The pungent smell of cordite was everywhere. There were cartridge cases scattered all over the floor and on the stairs. The door of our bedroom was riddled with bullet holes. She picked up one of the babies, took her downstairs and handed her to Lorraine, who had meanwhile followed

With the Wardrobe and the Bed Against the Door 59

her to my house. Then she went back up to the little girls' bedroom to get the other baby. She offered to take them home to sleep with her in her house and I consented. Anywhere, as long as it was far away from that house...

Before leaving, Brenda phoned the police once again, while Lorraine looked after the children. I was so distracted I wouldn't have been able to. Several minutes passed and no help had come. Brenda had to phone a second time, then a third time a few minutes later. It took some time before we heard the sound of an approaching RUC armoured car. By then it was too late. The men who had tried to kill us were miles away. Later on we found out that, to get to our house, they had opened a gap in the hedge separating our area from the loyalist district where they had come from. They took the same short cut when they left.

After a couple of hours I was taken to hospital suffering from severe shock. It took me a long time to recover. I never went back to live in that house. It's too dangerous to live next to a hedge that anyone at all can pass through simply because we have nobody to protect us when we're in danger. And yet, the police station is very close to our house, just at the corner of our street. That night the policemen had probably been able to hear the noise of the shooting quite clearly.

Things are very hard for me now. I burst into tears all the time and I have to take sleeping pills just to keep going.

Our present house is less comfortable and smaller than the one before. I miss my neighbours and my house in Springfield Road. Yet I can't go back to that street. After us, a very short time after, another family met with the same fate.

Taken from a written statement on the murder attempt on the McKenna family - July 28th, 1992

10.
I Have Received Death Threats
Rosemary Nelson – Lurgan (1998)

Odras was a woman so brave that she dared to stand up for her rights against Morrigan, the fearsome Goddess of Death. Odras possessed a cow which Morrigan wanted her own bull, Slemuin the Shining, to mount. So the goddess stole the cow and took it down to the underworld. Odras was furious at the loss of the animal and she went off to the wilds of Connacht, to Cruachan's Cave. But there she was bewitched and she fell fast asleep beneath the great magic oak trees. Morrigan returned to the surface of the earth and transformed the young maiden into a pool of water as punishment for her temerity.

***

Rosemary Nelson was an internationally known and respected human rights lawyer. She was murdered on March 15th, 1999, when a loyalist booby-trap bomb attached to her car exploded, severing both her legs and causing extensive abdominal injuries. She died hours later in hospital.

Rosemary Nelson was 40 years of age. She was a wife to Paul Nelson and a mother to Gavin (13), Christopher (11) and Sarah (8). She studied for her law degree at Queen's University, Belfast. After working for other solicitors for a number of years, she became the first female solicitor to open her own practice in her native town. The weekend immediately prior to her death marked the tenth 'birthday' of her practice.

She was obstructed in the execution of her professional duties in contravention of the United Nations Basic Principles on the Role of Lawyers. Despite the death threats issued against her by members of the RUC she was courageous. On September 29th 1998 she gave evidence to the International Operations and Human Rights Sub-committee of the US Congress. In her statement she highlighted the difficulties facing lawyers in Northern Ireland.

Her murder threatens the rule of law and all human rights defenders in Ireland.

***

I have been a solicitor in private practice in Northern Ireland for the past twelve years. My practice includes a mixture of several areas of law, including crime, matrimonial and personal injury cases. My clients are drawn from both sides of the community. For the last ten years I have been representing suspects detained for questioning about politically motivated offences. All of these clients have been arrested under emergency laws and held in specially designed holding centres. There are three such centres across Northern Ireland.

Since I began to represent such clients and especially since I became involved in a high profile murder case, I have begun to experience difficulties with the RUC. These difficulties have involved RUC officers questioning my professional integrity, making allegations that I am a member of a paramilitary group and, at their most serious, making threats against my personal safety, including death threats. All of these remarks have been made to my clients in my absence because lawyers in Northern Ireland are routinely excluded from interviews with clients detained in the holding centres.

This behaviour on the part of RUC officers has worsened during the last two years and particularly since I began to represent the residents of the Garvaghy Road, who have objected to an Orange Order march passing through their area from Drumcree Church. Last year I was present on the Garvaghy Road when the parade was forced through. I had been present on the road for a number of days because I had

62 Women's Stories from the North of Ireland

instructions from my clients to apply for an emergency judicial review of any decision allowing the parade to pass through the area. When the police began to move into the area in forces in the early hours of 5th July I went to the police lines and identified myself as a lawyer representing the residents. I asked to speak to the officer in charge. At that point I was physically assaulted by a number of RUC officers and subjected to sectarian verbal abuse. I sustained bruising to my arm and shoulder. The officers responsible were not wearing any identification numbers and when I asked for their names I was told to 'fuck off'. I complained about the assault and abuse but to date have obtained no satisfactory response from the RUC.

Since then my clients have reported an increasing number of incidents when I have been abused by RUC officers, including several death threats against myself and members of my family. I have also received threatening telephone calls and letters. Although I have tried to ignore these threats, inevitably I have had to take account of the possible consequences for my family and for my staff. No lawyer in Northern Ireland can forget what happened to Patrick Finucane nor dismiss it from their minds.

(...) I have also complained about these threats, again without any satisfactory response. Although complaints against the RUC are supervised by the Independent Commission for Police Complaints, the complaints themselves are investigated by RUC officers. Recently, a senior police officer from England has been called in to investigate my complaints in view of the RUC's apparent inability to handle my complaints impartially. This English police officer is interviewing witnesses himself and has decided not to rely on any assistance from the RUC.

I believe that one of the reasons that RUC officers have been able to indulge in such systematic abuse against me is that the conditions under which they interview clients

I Have Received Death Threats 63

detained under emergency laws allow them to operate without sufficient scrutiny. My access to my clients can be deferred for periods of up to 48 hours. I am never allowed to be present while my clients are interviewed. Interviews are now subject to silent video recording but are not yet being audio-recorded, although that is due to be introduced.

(...) Another reason why RUC officers abuse me in this way is because they are unable to distinguish me as a professional lawyer from the alleged crimes and causes of my clients. This tendency to identify me with my clients has led to accusations by RUC officers that I have been involved in paramilitary activity, which I deeply and bitterly resent.

(...) I believe that my role as a lawyer in defending the rights of my clients is vital. The test of a new society in Northern Ireland will be to the extent to which it can recognise and respect that role, and enable me to discharge it with without improper interference. I look forward to that day.

Washington, September 29th 1998

Extracts from Rosemary Nelson's statement before the International Operations and Human Rights Sub-committee of the US Congress.

11.
I'm a Solicitor and a Colleague of Pat Finucane
Padraigín Drinan - Belfast (1996)

In origin Eithne was a primeval Irish goddess who lived solely on the milk of a sacred cow of India. Eithne was watched over by a demon which drove off any man who dared to approach. She was assimilated into Celtic mythology as a Princess of the Fomorians, the first of the Irish Sea-Gods. Her tribe offered her to the Tuatha Dé Danann in an attempt to unify the two peoples. Eithne ('the Princess of the sweet hazel nuts') married Dian Céacht of the tribe of the Tuatha and gave birth to Lugh, the God of Light.

Another version tells of how Eithne was shut up in a high tower where no man could reach her. In fact, according to a prophecy, her sons were destined to murder their father. But a hero by the name of McKeenly, disguising himself as a woman, managed to gain access to her room and to sleep with her. He was to pay for his audacity with his life. Eithne's sons too met with a tragic fate; every one of them died in infancy.

***

I'm forty years old. I studied at the Queen's University, Belfast. I have been practicing law for twenty years. I live in Finaghy Road, a long road linking Lisburn Road to Andersonstown Road. The railway line divides Finaghy Road into two halves. I live in the section of the road which is inhabited mainly by unionists.

I work with many rape and crisis centres. These are centres for women who have been the victims of violence. My clients

I'm a Solicitor and a Colleague of Pat Finucane 65

come from both communities; these cases are referred to me by the Falls Women's Centre and the Shankill Road Women's Centre.

Over the last few years I have been concerned with human rights, especially those involving people being held in custody in the interrogation centres of Northern Ireland. At the end of the eighties, together with a number of other solicitors, I denounced the British government to the European Court of Human Rights in Strasbourg. In Northern Ireland a suspect can be held for up to seven days, in contravention of the European Convention on Human Rights. Another right I have always defended is the right of Irish prisoners to be treated in accordance with the standards enshrined in international law. In many cases the treatment reserved for them is far more harsh.

In the past I had the opportunity to work with Pat Finucane. Pat was a very prominent lawyer. He was murdered in front of his wife and children by loyalist gunmen on February 12th 1989. His death was a terrible tragedy. He was killed because he had denounced the actions of the British authorities in Northern Ireland to the European Court of Human Rights. He vigorously maintained that, even in situations of conflict, the rule of law must prevail and that the law must be applied in equal measure to all. He had, in fact succeeded in taking members of the police and the army to court for having broken the law and for being involved in the killing of ordinary citizens in disputed circumstances. This made Pat a victim of the illegal, undemocratic system which he had so often denounced. Pat had become a serious threat in the eyes of the British establishment; that is why he was killed.

We, his colleagues, are well aware that what happened to him could happen to any of us. In fact many of us have been intimidated or have received death threats.

Ten years ago, when I first came to live in Finaghy Road, I discovered to my cost that I was the first and only Catholic resident in the area. One day, by pure chance, someone noticed that my car had been tampered with. If I had turned the ignition key I would have been blown to bits. Even now, ten years later, I still can't describe what I felt when I realised that, in the blink of an eye, I could have been dead. Some time afterwards part of my house was set on fire. It was a way of forcing me to get out of the neighbourhood. Though I was extremely frightened, I concluded that I would manage to survive where I was if I took the necessary precautions. So I made up my mind to stay.

I have also received death threats. It was when I was involved in the case of some women who had been raped by members of a paramilitary loyalist group, the Ulster Defence Association. The UDA did not want my clients to bring charges against the perpetrators of these acts of violence. Therefore, as their solicitor, I was repeatedly threatened. The UDA even planted bombs in places where they thought I might be going. The situation had become almost unendurable for me.

For someone not living in Northern Ireland it is not easy to understand that, even if you escape with your life, something inside of you withers and dies. Such is the terror you feel that, afterwards, when it is all over, you are not the person you were. That is precisely what happened to me at the beginning of the summer this year.

On the evening of July 8th, at about 8 o'clock, I was at home. For the previous two days thousands of Orangemen had been gathering in Portadown. Their rallying point was a large open field in front of the church of Drumcree. They were protesting against the police ban on their planned march down the nationalist Garvaghy Road. There were hundreds of policemen on the scene. Tension grew with each passing hour. I was not aware that the Belfast Orangemen had begun to concentrate their forces in Lower Ormeau Road. Nor did I know that notices had been put up at all the bus stops telling them to meet every evening in the same street.

I'm a Solicitor and a Colleague of Pat Finucane 67

Then somebody told me what was going on. I had to leave the house that evening. I knew that the police would isolate some of the streets in our area in order to allow the protest to take place. As I had no intention of letting myself be blockaded inside my own house, I decided to leave as soon as I could. But I had left it too late. The Orangemen's march, with its police escort, had already left the unionist area, which was fairly close to where I live. Some of the marchers had been made to follow a route which took them over the railway bridge and they had already reached the small nationalist area in which I live. By the time the police began to seal off our streets so as to prevent anyone entering, dozens of Orangemen had already filtered into the area near my house.

I peeped out of the window to see what was going on. There were about two hundred of them and they were not just youths. This fact was particularly frightening. The crowd halted in front of my house; they were probably unsure as to what to do next. After a short time they pushed open the gate, entered my garden and started to walk slowly round and round the house. I was all alone. As soon as I saw them coming I sat down on the top step of the stairs leading up to the bedroom and grabbed the phone. I soon realised that they could see me quite clearly through the glass door. I sat there, paralysed, in total silence. They looked at me and I stared back at them. There were about twenty of them. I was powerless to do anything. At that moment I was really convinced they would kill me. My thoughts ran wild, jostling one another in my brain. I was now panic-stricken, incapable of thinking straight. I thought of Pat Finucane, of the houses which had been recently attacked, of the death threats I had received. The torment seemed endless.

For a whole hour and a half nobody moved. My house was completely surrounded. The Orangemen were getting their instructions over a mobile phone. RUC men paced to and fro on the footpath. An RUC jeep positioned itself in front of my house and some policemen carrying guns came into my

68 *Women's Stories from the North of Ireland*

garden. No one, however, was made to get off my property. The fact that I had my phone with me was a great comfort. It served to keep me from panicking. At least someone knew what was happening to me. I did not recognise any of the people I could see. Later on I was told that some of them were members of a paramilitary loyalist group.

Looking back, I do not think that their primary objective was to frighten me. What they really wanted was to exercise their right to enter, undisturbed, a nationalist property which happened to be located in a predominantly unionist area. As for the refusal of the police to take action, they had probably decided not to intervene; they knew who lived in that house. The police did not, in fact, simply escort the Orange marchers. Quite the contrary, they formed an integral part of the group which arrived in my area. I watched them as they took their orders from the marchers with the mobile phones. The police arrived on the scene and left it when they were told to. They made not the slightest effort to break up the crowd, nor did they behave as one would expect stalward guardians of law and order to behave.

Meanwhile, a friend of mine had tried to come to my aid. Because of the road blocks, however, she did not succeed. When she was only yards away from my house she saw a man in a car approaching the zone which had been isolated by the police. This man was stopped immediately by the Orangemen. They beat him and kicked him as the police stood by and watched. She heard the man shouting, 'I'm a Protestant! I'm a Protestant!', but to no avail. My friend implored the group to leave him alone. It was no use. Even after he had lost his senses they went on kicking him. She ran to the policemen who were escorting the marchers to inform them that the man was going to die if nobody came to save him. They replied that they had orders not to intervene. She got the same answer when she rushed to the nearest police station to tell them what was going on and to ask for help. In

I'm a Solicitor and a Colleague of Pat Finucane 69

desperation, she contacted the local priest. He called the police straight away, but he got the same reply.

Mine was not the only house to be surrounded. I managed to get through to my next-door neighbours on the phone. They told me they had had to stretch out on the floor and pretend there was nobody at home. After a while the crowd dispersed. Several hours passed before I was able to calm myself. I was truly terrified. All that time I had been quite sure that, in a matter of minutes, I was going to be killed.

Two months have gone by since that event and I still find it hard to talk about it. I am fully aware of what would have happened if the Orangemen had decided to break down the door and enter the house. The police had, in fact, received explicit orders not to intervene. At times, when things are not going well, I blame myself for what happened. I suppose I should have seen it coming, considering the work I do. I tell myself that I should have moved to another neighbourhood after the death of Pat Finucane. But then I calm down and I realize that the blame for what happened does not lie with me.

Episodes of this kind make my job even more difficult. Fear is always lurking there in the shadows; I am never quite without fear. And yet I know I must go on – for myself, for Pat and for all my colleagues.

Recorded in Belfast, August 1996

Following the murder of Rosemary Nelson in March 1999, Paidrigín Drinan has become the legal representative of the residents of Garvaghy Road, in Portadown. Despite the fact that she has received new death threats, the police authorities have refused to provide her with personal protection. In September 2000 the Loyalist Volunteer Force (LVF), a loyalist paramilitary group, published a 'Death List' on the worldwide web. The list contains the names of 200 people on whom the LVF have pronounced the death sentence. Paidrigín Drinan's name is on that list.

12.
Seven Days of Ill-Treatment
Geraldine O'Connor – Belfast (1991)

Caer - 'Yew Berry' - was a young virgin swan who lived on a lake in Ireland called Loch Béal Dragan' (the lake of the Dragon's Mouth). She used to swim wearing a necklace consisting of one hundred and fifty rows of golden spheres. Aonghus, the king of poets, saw her and he fell in love. Caer enticed him into the lake and Aonghus was transformed into a swan. In this form the two of them winged their way towards Brugh na Bóinne (the megalithic ritual site just north of Tara). As they flew they sang so sweetly that all the people of the island wept for three whole days.

***

I'm twenty-nine. I'm separated and I have two children: a girl of seven and a boy of ten. Up to a short time ago I lived in Beechmount Drive, off the Falls Road in Belfast. But now I have no fixed abode.

It all began at half past six one morning in June 1991. I was woken up by a banging on the front door, followed by the pounding of heavy footsteps up the stairs getting nearer and nearer. I hadn't the time to get out of my bed before an RUC policeman burst into my room. In a harsh voice he told me to follow him right away. 'What's going on?', I asked him. I was still half asleep. 'We've got to search the house', came the reply. So I got dressed and I went downstairs. There I found a group of British soldiers all ready to start the search. They were carrying fire-axes and other pieces of heavy-duty equipment.

Seven Days of Ill-Treatment   71

I realised I should go and call someone. The thought of my two children and myself being left alone in the hands of these men, without anybody knowing, terrified me. But the soldiers wouldn't let me leave the house. So I told my son to run and call his grandfather, who lived nearby. When my father arrived he was told that I had been arrested under Article 14 of the Prevention of Terrorism Act. I knew that law very well and I knew what it meant: to be taken to Castlereagh and held there for seven days. I barely had time to hand the kids over to my father before I was forced to leave with the policemen.

Castlereagh is the most feared Interrogation Centre in Northern Ireland. When we got there I was shut up in a windowless room. The furniture consisted of a bunk and a chair which was bolted to the floor. They ordered me to make the bed and I obeyed. I didn't know what time it was for I had lost all count of time. I couldn't believe what was happening. I was in a state of confusion and shock. Everything had happened so fast: the hammering on the door, the policemen in my bedroom, the house search, my children left all alone, the terror of what was still to come...

They brought me breakfast – uneatable it was. Then they took me to see a doctor, who examined me. This is standard practice every morning in an Interrogation Centre, to check on the detainee's physical condition. After that I was taken back to my cell. I tried to keep calm but I was very nervous. I had heard about lots of people being taken to Castlereagh and being subjected to ill-treatment for seven days. Still, I kept telling myself that in my case it would be different because I had done nothing wrong.

My thoughts were interrupted by the arrival of a man and a woman, both plain-clothes police officers. They took me to a room nearby to subject me to what they euphemistically call an 'interview'. When they asked me for information about myself, I told them I would only talk in the presence of a lawyer. I knew that the only information that I was obliged to

72 *Women's Stories from the North of Ireland*

give was my name and address. No more. This is a rule that everyone in the nationalist community knows by heart because it can happen to anyone to be hauled off to Castlereagh. You must try not to say a word, nor sign any documents. The police could always add on false statements and so turn anything with your name on it into a self-incriminating confession. They asked me who my lawyer was. When I told them, they said: 'Another IRA sympathiser! He'll soon wind up in a body-bag like Pat Finucane!'

I had to submit to six 'interviews' that day, but I managed to remain silent all the time. They kept asking me: 'Do you drink a lot of coffee in your house?' I couldn't make sense of the question, so they explained. They were referring to coffee bombs, rudimentary little bombs that the IRA made using Nescafè jars filled with explosives. When they went off, they had the same effect as a real grenade.

'Who do you know in the IRA? Are you a member of the IRA?' To hear them talk you'd have thought I had taken part in a thousand IRA actions and had spent my whole life carrying out terrorist attacks. The questions came thick and fast, like machine-gun fire but I didn't talk. This really got up their noses.

That's when the ill-treatment and the sexual abuse began. Even now I find it hard to talk about it. Yet I force myself to, in the hope that it may help other women who might find themselves in the same position as mine. They started off by hitting me on the back of the neck and yelling into my ear. A policeman sat down in front of me and spread my legs apart. Then he rubbed his elbow hard against my sex while the others were hitting me. They held me in that position for nearly two hours.

One of them kept sucking peppermint sweets while he was questioning me. All of a sudden, he got mad because I wouldn't answer his questions and he spat all the sweets into my face. During another 'interview' that same policeman pressed my lower jaw down for a couple of seconds, then,

Seven Days of Ill-Treatment 73

without warning, he rammed my chin upwards. I felt as if my teeth were shattering as they smashed against each other. Another time he kissed me really hard on the lips and there was nothing I could do to stop him. His partner was just as bad. In one of the numberless 'interviews', he put his arms around me and caressed my thighs over and over, asking me if it excited me.

For hours at a time all this was accompanied by shouts and insults of a sexual nature. 'You know why your husband left you? Because you're ugly. Who'd go for a woman like you? You're so ugly you probably had sex only a couple of times in your whole life; that's why you've only got two kids. Fancy a quickie, even if you are as ugly as sin?"

They kept making jeering remarks about my hair and my clothes. The morning they burst into the house I had pulled on the first things I could lay my hands on: a pair of jeans and a heavy jumper which I never took off because it helped to deaden the pain of the beatings. So they said: 'Haven't you got anything else to wear? That sweater's disgusting; it stinks... See if you can change it before the next interview'. And every time I came into the interview room they'd hold their noses because of the smell coming from me, according to them.

Several times they referred to my children: 'We've already handed them over to the social workers, so they can have a family at last. You won't have them with you ever again. At first I didn't believe them because I knew I had left the children with my father. But they repeated it so many times that I wasn't sure about anything and I ended up believing them.

Sometimes there were as many as nine 'interviews' in one day. They began at eight in the morning and went on till half past midnight. There were eight members in the interrogation team, operating in pairs and working in relays. An 'interview' lasted an hour and a half on average. When it was over, I was taken back to my cell for ten minutes and then handed over to the next pair of interrogators.

74 Women's Stories from the North of Ireland

For seven days they went on beating me on the head and back. They hit me in the face, kicked me, threatened to hang me and give me electric shocks. They yelled repeatedly into my ears: 'You're an IRA whore! You screw all of them, one after the other, don't you?' One day a policewoman who was standing behind me while I was sitting down kept tapping me on the head with the end of a pen. Later I was told that this kind of repeated action causes an excessive amount of fluid to be secreted in order to protect the brain. This can cause cerebral lesions and yet leave no visible marks. Still not satisfied, this woman put two fingers under my chin and kept my head pushed back for an interminable length of time. Whenever I tried to lower my chin she pushed it back up again and screamed into my ear.

I had my arm in a cast at that time as the result of a fracture. They kept hitting the cast till they broke the plaster; then they used adhesive tape to hold it together.

Every morning I informed the doctor about the ill-treatment I had been subjected to but he gave no sign of being interested. One day he told me that the Chief Inspector had been present at the 'interview'. According to him, nothing of what I had reported had actually taken place.

I was held in solitary confinement all the time I was in Castlereagh. I was put in the last room at the end of a corridor, with no one in the cell next door. After the first two days they allowed me to meet with my lawyer. This was my only contact with the outside world, once every twenty-four hours.

Fear never left my side… I was terrified at the idea that, sooner or later, they would break down my resistance with their beatings. I had heard of people who had not been able to hold out in the face of beatings and threats. In the end they had signed false, self-incriminating statements or made verbal confessions extracted under duress. This way, many totally innocent people had been convicted. They were now serving lengthy terms of imprisonment in Long Kesh. I thought of what it would mean for me to be separated from

Seven Days of Ill-Treatment 75

my children for all that time. Who would take care of them? I prayed and prayed to God to give me the strength to resist and stay mute. He must have heard me because the seventh day came and I had still not uttered a word.

They informed me that I was to be charged with murder. Later on, the charge was gradually reduced: first to 'attempted murder', then 'conspiring to commit a murder', 'IRA membership' and finally 'harbouring IRA members'. When they told me they would let me go and that we'd be seeing one another the next day in court, I didn't believe them. You see, during all that time they had told me nothing but lies. Yet it was true. I was ordered to gather up my belongings, then they escorted me out into the courtyard. They put me into a yellow van and took me to Musgrave Street Police Station to be charged.

The next morning in court, the magistrate decided that I was to be remanded in custody in Maghaberry Prison, pending trial. When I got to the jail I had to submit to a strip-search like all the other prisoners. It was a female warder, not a doctor, who removed my cast.

Back in my cell I had the feeling that time had come to a standstill; the hours never seemed to pass. And yet I was in Maghaberry for no more than twenty-four hours. My lawyer had hinted at the possibility of a judicial review. I hadn't the faintest idea of what the term meant. He had been very active and had succeeded in securing my parole. I would have to report to the police twice a week until the date of my trial.

When I was released, I decided I wouldn't go back home. I would spend the night with my parents. I couldn't wait to see my children again. It was a decision that saved my life. For people who don't live here it's hard to understand that in Northern Ireland being alive or dead, being allowed to live with your family or being thrown into jail for ten or twenty years, depends on mere chance. It can all depend on whether you take one decision rather than another on the spur of the moment, on whether you decide to go out or stay at home.

76 Women's Stories from the North of Ireland

So it happened that, while I was still at my parents' home, some men broke into my house with every intention of killing me. They were members of the paramilitary loyalist group the Ulster Freedom Fighters (UFF), as I found out later. It was my father who noticed that something was up, when he saw what they had done to my front door. When he told me on the phone, I reckoned it must have been the soldiers during one of their house searches. I didn't give it much thought. I went home and stayed inside the whole day.

At half past five that evening, however, the police returned to pay me a visit. 'My God!' I thought, 'they're here to arrest me again!' But all they did was ask me if someone had broken into my house. When I said no, they began to search the whole house including the back garden. I felt relieved. This time they wouldn't take me away. As for the search, well I figured it was routine procedure for people on parole. It was only later that evening that I realised what had really happened. When I came back home after visiting my sister, I found my brother waiting for me on the doorstep. 'Geraldine, you can't stay here any more. It was the UFF... They were going to kill you'. I didn't even cross the threshold. I was shocked and incredulous. Try as I might, I couldn't imagine why they would want to kill me.

The next morning the police cleared up my doubts; a note had been left at my front door telling me to contact the Grovenor Road Police Station. On the phone I was told that the BBC offices had received a message from the UFF: 'We have raided a house in the Beechmount area with the intention of killing Geraldine O'Connor. Like any man or woman who supports the republican movement, she will become a target for us...'

What on earth had happened? How could they consider me so dangerous to decide to kill me? I was distraught. Then, all of a sudden, a thought flashed across my mind and my blood froze; the phone call to the BBC had been made at 3 p.m., but the police had come to warn me only some hours

Seven Days of Ill-Treatment 77

later. They had not come immediately after the call because they wanted to give the UFF plenty of time to kill me. That was why they had arrived on the scene only when they were sure they would find me dead.

Today, one month after that nightmare experience, I have been acquitted on every count. And yet I feel I'm no longer the person I was. I used to be a single mother raising her kids and leading a normal life. Not any more. I feel a deep resentment towards what the police can do to anybody at all. They can ill-treat, humiliate, degrade any human being, without having to answer to anyone. They can come into our houses and take us away whenever they like. They can stand by impassively and pretend they know nothing when our lives are in danger. Many, many people in West Belfast have experienced what I went through. Among them there are youths and women living alone with their children. The police know these are the most vulnerable people, the ones on whom they can exert the greatest physical and psychological pressure.

I'm often stopped in the street and searched by either the RUC or the soldiers. The children get frightened and start crying. If I see a uniform in the distance, I try to hide in a shop or else I dodge down a side street.

My eldest boy can understand what's going on, even though I haven't said anything to him. He keeps on saying: 'We were lucky, weren't we?' One day he came back home with a friend. They were carrying bits of timber, small iron bars and other stuff they had picked up in the road. My son arranged them across the bottom of the front door and they said: 'Now they won't be able to take you away ever again'. In his own way, he's trying to protect me.

I'm never going back to my old house. I'm too frightened. I'm waiting to be assigned another house. I owned the house I lived in before. I suppose I could sell it now, but who'd buy it? Everyone here knows that if they want to kill you, the loyalists can come back more than once. In the past, nothing

78   *Women's Stories from the North of Ireland*

used to scare me. I always had some Protestant friends and I used to go out with them every now and then. Now I don't see them any more. I'm just not able to trust anybody.

Every night I sleep with the children in a different house. They're beginning to feel the strain of not having a house of their own any more. Things are getting very tough for me as well. Before I had a job, but I had to give it up because there were some Protestants working alongside me. With no house and no work I can make no plans for the future. Sometimes I think I'll have to leave Northern Ireland, maybe go south or abroad. But where? I asked my son and he replied: 'Some place where the police can't come and take you away...'

Recorded in Belfast, August 1991

13.
Sign, or You'll Never See Your Mother Again

Bridget Coogan – Belfast (1991)

Bé Find was tall and beautiful. This supernatural woman came from the 'Land of the Virgins', the Isle of Women, not far off the western coasts of Ireland. According to some legends she was a queen in the underworld, the patroness of all pleasures. Wherever she went she was surrounded by magical birds and she knew all the secrets of healing. Another legend tells of how she had come from her enchanted island to live with the King of the Isle of Man. He soon revealed himself to be a brutal husband and, rather than put up with his savage cruelty, she returned to her own home. The King followed her there and killed her.

***

I'm forty-eight years old. I'm a widow, with a son and a daughter. We live in Beechmount, just off Falls Road in West Belfast. My husband died when Liam was two years old and his sister five. I was still very young when I started working. Since then all I've ever done is work and bring up the children.

Three months ago my whole life changed. It was the first of May 1991. That morning the IRA had thrown a crude bomb at an RUC patrol who were carrying out a search in our area. One policeman was badly hurt. He died the next day.

At half past ten that evening the police and the soldiers came to our street. My son Liam wasn't home at the time. He'd gone out with his sister to rent a film at the video shop just over the road. When he came out of the shop a

80 *Women's Stories from the North of Ireland*

policeman rushed at him and threw him up against the wall yelling, 'Murderer! Now we're going to take you to Castlereagh and you won't be let out for the rest of your days!' Another soldier grabbed his arm and twisted it up behind his back so savagely that Liam's sister thought they wanted to break it. A third soldier took him by the hair and dragged him away. Then they shoved him into an RUC armoured car. My daughter begged them in tears to let him go, but it was no use. One of the soldiers turned around and pointed at her: 'You Irish whore, you!', he shouted. 'Next time it'll be your turn!'

Then the armoured car roared off. All that long way from Falls Road to the Castlereagh Interrogation Centre they kept on hitting Liam and punching him up. They had stripped off his leather jacket and they covered his head with it so he couldn't see anything.

It was just after midnight when the soldiers and the police came to my house. They stayed there till four in the morning. They went through all my personal belongings. They photographed every room and took measurements. 'That way, next time, we'll know the exact layout of every room', they told me. They turned Liam's room inside out and they took away everything he owned, including his dirty linen. They only thing they didn't notice was the ring I gave him last year. It's all I have left of him now. All I could do was stand by helpless and watch them tearing up the place. One of the soldiers asked me if the house was mine. I looked him straight in the eye and I said: 'I thought it was mine. But how can that be when you can just came in whenever you like, wreck it and take away my son?'

In the meantime, in Castlereagh, a nightmare was just starting for Liam. It was the same for three of his friends who had been arrested after him: Mark Prior and Jim McCabe, both nineteen, and Kevin Mulholland, who was seventeen. For seven whole days those four teenagers were subjected to

Sign, or You'll Never See Your Mother Again 81

physical violence and psychological pressure, from eight in the morning till half past midnight, with just two short breaks. During these 'interviews' Liam was hit in the belly, on the head and on the ear over and over by no less than eight men. Several times they held him by the hair and grabbed his throat so they nearly choked him. They squeezed his testicles hard and bawled obscenities at him about his sister and me. And then more slaps, punches and kicks.

Liam and his three friends couldn't stand up under all this. After days and days of abuse they ended up signing a self-incriminating statement that the police had already prepared. But it wasn't only the beatings that made them give in. Psychological blackmail and threats turned out to be very effective weapons against those scared kids. In order to get Liam to sign, they told him I had got very ill and that his sister had been taken to Castlereagh as well. They also convinced him that I had given the police a note begging him to sign for his sister's sake. Kevin Mulholland was a diabetic so they told him he'd have to do the same if he wanted to have his daily insulin shot which they had hurriedly taken from his house when they arrested him. Then there was the blackmailing of Jim McCabe and Mark Prior. They were both told that one of their parents had had a heart attack; if they wanted to see them for the last time they had better sign the statements incriminating themselves.

I was never allowed to see Liam for seven days. I was desperate. Two days after the arrest I met Kevin Winters, he lawyer, and I asked him what he thought of my son. He said that after talking to him for five minutes, he realised that Liam was innocent. In the case of all four boys the beatings and the threats had worked like a sort of brain-washing, so they ended up being persuaded they had actually done something wrong. After a week they were taken to the Grosvenor Road Police Station, where they were formally charged with murder.

82 Women's Stories from the North of Ireland

When I saw Liam again I found myself facing a different person: a terrified, trembling boy, with eyes that stared into space and sunken cheeks, who kept asking if his sister was all right. It's been three months now and Liam is awaiting trial for murder. If he's found guilty, he'll have to spend twenty years in prison.

Of the more than twenty youths arrested in Beechmount and Ballymurphy and locked up in Castlereagh that May day, not one had ever been in trouble with the police.

I have been living in a nightmare for months. My only support is the company of other mothers, sisters and relatives who are going through the same experience. We have set up a group called 'The Voice of the Innocent'. We want people to know about what happened to our sons. We hope someone will help us to get them out of jail and keep others from meeting with the same fate.

The youths in our area are always being stopped in the street, searched, attacked, insulted and beaten up by policemen and British soldiers. This often happens several times in just one day. The Castlereagh Interrogation Centre is only the final link in a chain of ill-treatment that they are subjected to every single day. Since they aren't able to arrest those responsible for the IRA attacks, the police just strike out blindly. They round up young boys and force them to sign incriminating statements so that they can show that those responsible have been found.

Our group has appealed to leading politicians and church organizations (not only in Ireland but also in the United States), as well as to the United Nations. A spokesperson for Amnesty International has come to see us, to gather direct testimony of what happened to our boys.

People in my area are very supportive; there are always young mothers, elderly folk and lots of Liam's friends standing by to lend a hand, making photocopies, cutting out newspaper articles, making phone calls. Every week the

Sign, or You'll Never See Your Mother Again 83

Andersonstown News, our local paper, prints a photograph of Liam and the other three boys, showing the number of days they have spent in jail so far – the same as for the Birmingham Six.

Since Liam was taken away, the rhythm of my days is marked out by my visits to the prison. I go to visit him twice a week for half an hour. On Tuesday and Friday mornings I get into the little van that leaves Falls Road taking us, the parents and relatives of the prisoners, to Long Kesh jail. On the way I exchange a few words with the mothers, the sisters and the girl-friends of the prisoners. There are always kids with us, some really little, with their feeding bottles and their nappies that have to be changed as soon as we get to the prison.

When I'm home alone I find myself looking out of the window at groups of young boys walking in the street and it seems to me that I can see Liam there with them. Sometimes, without thinking, I lean over the gate like I used to, to see if he's coming up from the end of the road. Sometimes, after I've done the shopping, I discover that I've bought some things that only Liam likes.

When I walk past the policemen patrolling the area, or soldiers stationed against the wall of my house with their guns levelled at the passers-by, they always stare at me. They know who I am. It's the sort of look I'd see if somebody ripped my heart out and, after smashing it to pulp, stood there observing my reaction. But I'm not afraid. I could stand in front of them and look them straight in the eye and not say a word even if the beat me to death.

Recorded in Belfast, August 1991

14.
Cockroaches and Mice
Martina Anderson – Derry (1988)

According to the Irish legend, Bé Chuma - 'Goddess of the magic vessel' - was among the earliest divinities of the island, known as the Tuatha Dé Danann, the People of the Goddess Danu. She dwelt in the heart of the island, on the enchanted hill of Tara. If a king shared her bed, he would rule all Ireland. The Tuatha Dé Danann shunned her for her behaviour, but they were powerless to alter the course of history; the kings remained and the Tuatha Dé Danann were defeated.

***

A chara,

Conditions in here are deteriorating rapidly. The place is infested with cockroaches and the mice are becoming a regular feature. Last week I was on the wash-up with one of the women. She pulled out the tray of the toaster and in the process decapitated a mouse. You can imagine the sight! Another one crawled through one of the women's hair in bed last week.

To add to that the food is appalling; is it any wonder we're all losing weight? Most days we live on toast and jam. When that happened with the toaster we wouldn't use for a day or so hoping it would be cleaned, but hunger got the better of us and we cleaned it as best we could ourselves.

The worst has yet to come. The building is so old that the sluice can no longer manage our body waste. So, from Wednesday 27th January till Tuesday 9th February the sluice overflowed on four mornings and the urine etc. made its way

Cockroaches and Mice 85

out onto the area where we eat. This has been happening for years and rather than accept the fact that the building is falling down round us (after all it is 180 years old), the Assistant Governor has tried to put the responsibility onto us women.

Thankfully we are not as thick as he must think we are. It is bad enough that I have to stay in this cell for twelve hours with my own body waste in a pot, but it's worse when I empty it in the sluice and that overflows, and up to 38 women's body waste comes up round the area when breakfast is served! The Assistant Governor put a notice on the board saying: 'The main reson for this flooding is that inmates are throwing items into the sluice which are not intended to go there'. One of these items stated is 'sanitary towels'... In all other women's prisons sanitary towel disposal bags are made available but they are not here, so he must want the women to keep the used sanitary towels on their locker till morning. He has a cheek to use the word 'unhygienic'. Of course what we want to know is what the men in Wandsworth are doing with sanitary towels because their sluice overflows too!

Anyway, not only do we have a wash-up list on a rota basis, but from now on there will be a 'shit list' on a rota basis where inmates 'will be instructed to clean up'. To date there had been one mop and bucket, and the rest was collected in cloths down on hands and knees and no disinfection for later. Breakfast is served with the collected buckets of dirt at the side of the breakfast queue. They have promised more mops and buckets but as far as I'm concerned it's not my problem. I'm 'held' here. I don't live here. If I was held in better conditions I would be more responsive but not when I'm living in dirt, eating dirt, seeing dirt and thinking dirt.

Martina Anderson;
D 25134
H Wing; Durham Prison; February 15th 1988

15.
Strip-Searches
Karen Quinn – Belfast (1992)

Lí Ban was the daughter of the god Eochaidh. One day Eochaidh ran off with his stepmother and neglected to perform the sacred rites, thereby arousing the anger of the other gods. As punishment for his behaviour all his lands were flooded and all the people were drowned, save for Lí Ban and her little dog. For the next three hundred years the two of them lived together at the bottom of the lake which had been formed by the flood. In the end they turned into sea creatures: Lí Ban became a salmon and her little dog became an otter. One day Lí Ban got curious about what was happening on land and so she let herself be caught in a fisherman's net. Taken ashore, the goddess assumed the form of a beroch (mermaid) who was always accompanied by an otter. But one day a cruel man killed the otter and the goddess, bereft now of her life-long companion, turned back into human form and died. To this day Lí Ban haunts the oceans in the form of a lonely sea bird.

***

I'm thirty-four and I have four children. I'm serving a nine-year sentence in Maghaberry. It is a modern, maximum-security prison equipped with sophisticated surveillance systems. Back in 1986, all the women of the old Armagh Prison were transferred here.

On Monday morning, March 9th, 1992, I woke up early like every morning and waited for the warders to come and open the security locks on the cell doors. But at half past eight we were all still locked in. I was told that that morning there was going to be a general search. I knew what that meant: sniffer dogs and squads of prison guards for special checks. I wasn't particularly worried.

Soon after, I looked out the window and I saw a group of guards, male and female, going into another wing of the prison. They were wearing helmets with visors and they were carrying shields. The prison authorities knew that the prisoners would not accept this kind of degrading search and so the guards, in anti-riot gear, had been sent, to carry out the strip-search by force. A couple of minutes later I heard screams of pain coming from the wing opposite ours; the strip-searches were under way.

I spent hours sitting there weeping, compelled to listen to what women just like me were having to go through. The screams didn't stop the whole day. The male members of the staff never left our block. I could hear them laughing all the time as they took it out on the women prisoners. It was terrible trying to fill in the time before my own turn came. Sooner or later I would have to submit to the same treatment.

In the evening, the female warders came into my cell. They ordered me to undress but I refused. Then they at jumped me. I tried to put up a fight but there wasn't much I could do to hold off those four women in riot gear when they set on me and pinned me down so I couldn't move a muscle. I was thrown down on the ground so hard that my face smacked against the floor. They twisted my arms violently up behind my back. Then they started to strip me.

I struggled as hard as I could. When they tried to pull my sweater off, it got stuck over my head and I couldn't breathe. Instinctively, I raised my chin. Again they slammed my face onto the floor and one of the warders kept it pressed down with her knee. My arms were twisted so far back that I thought they'd break. I yelled that I was having my period but that didn't stop them. Then I tried to press my tummy against the floor as hard as I could so they wouldn't be able to pull my trousers off. They grabbed me by the hips and managed to get the trousers down below my waist and then they yanked them roughly down over my ankles. The material

88 Women's Stories from the North of Ireland

rasped like a scrubbing-brush down my legs which I was still desperately pressing against the floor. I couldn't breathe for the pain. I was in a state of panic, with my arms pinned back behind me and the guard's knee pressing down on my head.

In the end they managed to strip me naked. As I lay there on the ground they threw me a blanket and a sanitary napkin. The warder who had held me down with her knee wasn't satisfied yet, though. So, as she was leaving, she landed me a violent kick in the ribs.

Throughout the strip-search the cell door had been left open and the guards stood about outside in the corridor. One of them leaned into the cell, looked me over carefully and told me to go to the association room because they had to search the cell. I was trembling at the thought of having to walk half naked between two lines of guards who had certainly heard everything that had been done to me. It was just too humiliating, so I refused. Once again it was the helmeted warders who dragged me out and carried me off.

I found myself in the association room. For me it was inconceivable that women could so brutally attack other women. The right side of my face was all puffed up; my eye was so swollen I could barely see and so was my jaw. My feet, my ankles and my knees were swollen too.

They brought me back to my cell and I waited for the doctor, who came after about ten minutes. He was shocked when he saw what they had done to me. He said that maybe my jaw had been broken but that he couldn't be sure as it was too swollen up. I'd have to be taken to the hospital the next morning for an X-ray. He prescribed some medicine for me and told me to put up with the pain as best I could.

That night I was still in shock. I wasn't able to cry or even to feel anything. I felt devastated. I spent hours sitting on the end of my bed just staring into space. When the dawn came, I still couldn't believe what they had done to me.

The X-rays showed nothing; there was no fracture, but the right side of my face, still swollen, was one massive blue-black bruise from my eye down to my chin. My whole body

Strip-Searches 89

was aching and covered in welts. And yet none of the warders, none of the prison staff commented on my bruised, disfigured face though they couldn't possibly have failed to notice it. The only ones who asked me how I felt were the other victims of those brutal attacks.

When I returned to the prison the following morning, one of the warders who had attacked me was on duty again. I felt sick to my stomach at the sight of her; just a few hours before she had made me stand naked before her while my menstrual blood trickled down my legs. She was the one who should have been ashamed and embarrassed after what she had done to me. How could this woman, who had forcibly stripped twenty-one women, act as if nothing at all had happened when she came face to face with one of her victims?

Some days later the prison authorities accused me of disobeying an order. My punishment was the loss of my right to a reduction of my sentence.

I haven't seen my children for two weeks now. I don't want them to see me in this state, with my bruises still showing. They've got enough to cope with, having to grow up without their mother.

I feel as if I had been raped. The worst thing is the thought that I was helpless to do anything to protect myself from the warders. I know now that they can attack me again any time they feel like it. I feel a great resentment towards those women who carried out the strip-search, but also towards the people who ordered it to be carried out and those who just stood there watching and did nothing.

As the days go by we are all recovering physically. Our bruises are fading, but the memory of what we were forced to endure will not fade so quickly.

This account is taken from a letter smuggled out of Maghaberry Prison in March 1992. It was given by Karen Quinn's mother to Silvia Calamati during the Northern Ireland Human Rights Assembly conference, held in London in April 1992

16.
A Prison Within a Prison
Róisín McAliskey – Coalisland (1997)

Sadhbh was the wife of the mighty warrior Fionn mac Cumhaill. This Irish heroine had such a horror of all bloodshed that she died as a result of the cruelty shown by her husband in battle. According to the most celebrated legend, a jealous druid transformed Sadhbh into a fawn and so she was forced to give birth to her son in the woods. The child was born in human form but Samdhbh could not resist the desire to lick his forehead. As a result, a lock of hair, just like a fawn's, sprouted right there on his forehead. The baby was therefore called Oisín ('baby deer') and in Ireland he became a legendary poet.

***

The daughter of Bernadette Devlin McAliskey, Róisín was arrested on November 20th 1996. She was detained under emergency laws and interrogated for six days in Castlereagh Interrogation Centre. She was remanded in custody in London on the basis of an extradition warrant issued by the German authorities in connection with an IRA mortar attack on the British Army base in Osnabrück (Germany), in June 1996. On November 30th 1996 she was transferred to Belmarsh, a men's prison. However, in response to worldwide protests, she was transferred back to Holloway, a women's prison in London.

When arrested, Róisín McAliskey was about four months pregnant and suffering from various medical ailments, including asthma and an eating disorder; she was also severely underweight.

A Prison Within a Prison 91

As a Category A high security prisoner on remand, she was strip-searched twice a day, morning and evening, as well as before and after visits even though she had 'closed' visits, meaning that there was no possible physical contact between her and her visitor. Amnesty International was concerned that the strip-searching, especially in connection with her visits, might not be necessary for security purposes and might lead to cruel, inhuman and degrading treatment. She was also reportedly restricted to taking exercises on the roof of the prison. The conditions of her imprisonment, combined with a lack of appropriate medical assitance, meant that her health deteriorated. Hers became a high-risk pregnancy.

A world-wide campaign was launched on her behalf by Amnesty International and other human rights organizations. As a result of this action, a few days before she was due to give birth, she was allowed to leave the prison and was transferred to Whittington hospital in London. With police officers standing beside her twenty-four hours a day, she gave birth to a baby girl, Loinnir, on May 26th 1998. It was only because of the pressure of international public opinion that she was allowed to keep the baby with her. As a direct result of the harsh treatment she had been subjected to in prison, Róisín McAliskey, who was suffering from post-traumatic stress, had to be moved to a special department of Maudsley hospital, London.

On March 9th 1998 the British Home Secretary Jack Straw announced that the proceedings regarding the extradition to Germany had been suspended. Róisín McAliskey was released for health reasons after spending sixteen months in jail.

In the letter that follows, written just a few weeks before the birth of her daughter, she expresses her gratitude to all those people, in every part of the world, who supported the campaign for her release.

***

Firstly, myself and Seán, and my family, would like to thank everyone for their active support, and I would like to say what

92   *Women's Stories from the North of Ireland*

an overwhelming difference it makes to know that people do care, especially when surrounded by people who don't.

It's in a situation like this that you realise that it is the thought that really counts. When you are isolated from everyone, and everything that you do and say is watched and monitored, your thoughts are the only things that remain your own – which actually makes it hard to share them with anyone. So I hope you will excuse me if this is a bit dull and muted.

Although everyone knows what a prison is, I don't think anyone can imagine 'how' it is until they experience it. There are no colours – everything is white or beige – and there are no shapes. It's all straight lines and right angles. All smooth to touch. There are no smells and it's probably a relief that the food doesn't taste.

But the oddest thing is the noise. There is no natural noise; it's all metallic. Even voices don't sound natural. They lack the life of emotion or something.

And it's then that you really notice that what is really missing in prison is the beginning and the end of life: there are no children and no old people. There is no real laughter, or innocence, or wisdom, or need to care and comfort others.

But that's where thoughts make all the difference and remind you that life is not like this. And there is more to people than prison allows you to see and feel. It is the closed and controlled environment that leads to closed and biased minds.

Out of nearly 30 women with children in the prison, only two would sit in a room with me. But when I am treated like such a danger that I am put in a high-security male prison, why wouldn't they be fearful and object to having to associate with what is presented as a threat to the little they have for themselves?

There is a prison rule that prisoners cannot share, lend or give anything to other prisoners. So that while you are removed from your family and friends, you are prevented from building new relationships. But if you are an Irish prisoner in England they segregate you; they build a prison within a prison. With the men, they house them in an SSU (Special Secure Unit). And as they haven't got an SSU for females I get a human equivalent. With two 'shadow' officers accompanying me at all times. Human bookends, giving me my own prison within a prison.

The only problem is that there is no prison for thoughts. You cannot keep people from thinking and you cannot take a thought away from someone. So to know that I am in your thoughts makes such a difference for my thoughts and my heart that I hope you can imagine even a small part of the great lift it gives me knowing that I am only alone in the physical sense.

I am due a month from today and I am very aware that it is only through people making their thoughts known that I am being allowed to keep my baby.

So while thanking you for all the active support, I really want to thank everyone for their thoughts.

Róisín McAliskey
Holloway Prison - London

Letter published in An Phoblacht/Republican News, 15th May 1997, p. 12

17.
My Brother Bobby
Bernadette Sands – Belfast (1981)

Éadaoin was the powerful goddess of the tribe of the Dé Danann. She fell under the power of the Queen of the Fairies, Fuamnach, and was changed into a fly. Still in the grip of the spell, for seven long years she flew buzzing round and round the world. Then she fell into a cup and a woman swallowed her. Re-born in human form, she married the King of Ireland but then she took the King's brother as her lover. Then the King of the Fairies, Midhir, who wanted to bring Éadaoin back to the supernatural realm, assumed the form of her husband and surprised her in the company of her lover. He forced her to return home. There he reassumed his true form and carried her off to Brí Léith, the place where the sun sets. They say that the two of them still live there, happy and content.

***

It might sound a bit odd, but on the morning they came to tell us that he had died, everyone else in my family was on the brink of desperation. It was as if they had informed us that Bobby had been the victim of some sudden, unforeseeable road accident. But I, Bernadette Sands, Bobby's sister, I had been waiting for this news right from the start, from the moment my older brother had decided to begin his hunger-strike. Bobby had been given a fourteen-year prison sentence for what the British government defined as terrorism but what is, in actual fact, a struggle for liberty.

My Brother Bobby 95

He had made up his mind to starve himself to death unless his status as a political prisoner was recognised.

It had not been a hasty decision. Quite the opposite. He had thought things through very thoroughly and he had a clear view of the extreme consequences of his actions. And anyway, after four and a half years of protest, facing as he was the prospect of another ten years in prison, when every other means had been attempted, what else was there for the Irish political prisoners to do except to embark on a hunger strike and take it to, even beyond, the limits of human endurance? Bobby intended to blaze a trail, to make others understand that the supreme value of human life could be sacrificed in the name of even higher values: liberty and dignity.

And so, two days later, on May 7th 1981, as Bobby's funeral was taking place in Belfast, I was one of the one hundred thousand people who accompanied him to his final resting place. I was one of the many who did not weep; because by his strength, his determination, his courage, Bobby had bequeathed to me the determination to go on.

My father, John, and my mother, Rosaleen, met and married thirty years ago in Abbots Cross (Newtownabbey), in the northernmost suburb of Belfast. In March 1954 their first child, Bobby, was born. In April 1955 Marcella came along; in November 1958 it was my turn and their last child, John like his father, came into the world in the month of June 1962. By then the loyalists had already thrown us out of our home.

It was, in fact, just before John was born that the troubles began; most of our neighbours in the row of houses where we lived were Protestants. Some of them were members of the B-Specials. For Catholics, conditions were pretty rough most of the time. Until that day we managed to get by because everyone seemed to think that my mother, who was a very reserved person, was a Protestant. But then one day, my neighbours found out that we were not Protestants. The people next door took to banging on the walls at all hours of

96 *Women's Stories from the North of Ireland*

the day and night. If my mother went to hang out the washing, our neighbour would go out too and hang her washing on the same line. If she washed the windows, the woman next door would do the same, just to mock her. So every day my mother had to take Bobby, Marcella and me and traipse around Belfast for hours. This was the only way we could avoid being harassed by our neighbours. It also happened to be the best way for her to get a first-class nervous breakdown. Our doctor put his foot down: either our neighbours put an end to this torture, or we would have to move for the sake of my mother's health.

We packed up and left. For several months we stayed with uncles, aunts and relatives until my father managed to find a new home. And so we moved to Doonbeg Drive, Rathcoole, and set up house there in December 1961.

Bobby was seven at the time and he was a real scamp; during our holidays in Waterford he suddenly got bitten by the fishing bug. Off he would go to the pier every morning with his home-made fishing rod and a piece of cheese for bait; he used to catch an unbelievable amount of fish. He'd be back in the evening (we were living in a caravan) but when everyone was asleep he would sneak out with Marcella and they'd be off back to the pier. One night my mother woke and saw they weren't in their beds and she went looking for them. As soon as she found them she nearly skinned them alive. Do you think it did any good? Back they went the next night and the next and every night after. We hid the fish they caught under the caravan and after three days the stink began to infect the surrounding air. My mother discovered the trick and,   she taught both of them that the night-time was for sleeping and not for fishing.

But if our mother had a strong character, Bobby's was just as strong. When we did something wrong, we were chased out of the house and let back in only at supper-time. Whenever Bobby was sent out he refused to come back in; it

My Brother Bobby 97

was always my mother who caved in first and went out into the garden to coax him into coming in to supper. Nobody could beat him for stubbornness. If the other boys hit him, he gave as good as he got; he just never gave in. Maybe after he had turned the corner, he might break down and bawl like a baby, but he would never, ever let others see him cry.

So, when his ordeal began at Long Kesh, he never told anyone in the family about the beatings the guards gave him, about the endless days he spent in the punishment cell or of the times he had been ill and never properly looked after. He minimized everything and he never complained – even when he began to suffer terribly during the hunger strike, even when they had to put him into padded pyjamas to keep his bones from coming out through his skin with every move he made. Even then he didn't complain.

Bobby went to the Stella Maris primary school and then to the middle school in Rathcoole. When he completed his compulsory education he went to the local tech' and got work as an apprentice in a coach-building works in the industrial estate nearby. His first morning on the job he found three fellows standing by the factory gate, cleaning guns: 'You see these? Well, if you don't get out of here we're going to try them out on you', they said. But Bobby was hard-headed and he wasn't going to knuckle under. He went into the factory and they pointed out his locker to him. When he opened it, he found another invitation: 'Get out right now, if you value your life'. True to form, Bobby stayed put: for two years. At the end of this period, the manager sent for him and said: 'We're doing some re-structuring and we'll be making some staff cuts. As of tomorrow you'll be laid off'. The next day he found out that he was the only victim of the 're-structuring'. Out of all the employees in the firm the only one who got the sack was Bobby Sands.

Doonbeg Drive, where we had moved to in December 1961, was in a unionist area. In June 1972 we were again forced to

98 *Women's Stories from the North of Ireland*

pack up and leave, this time in a much more painful way than the last time. For a year and a half we were the target of increasing intimidation. We had made friends with lots of Protestant kids in the area and we used to go around with them, but things got so bad that we had to change our habits radically. When we saw the young thugs belonging to the tartan gangs on the street, the Protestant boys started going off on their own and the Catholic kids followed suit, until, one night, the Protestants virtually sealed off the whole area and the UDA, the Protestant militia, started marching down the streets and threatening the houses of Catholics. That evening there were no actual raids but it was clear that time was running out for us in that area.

The unionist circles were very worried and they put it out that our road, the main road in Rathcoole, harboured the highest concentration of Catholic families; in fact there were six of us. But the stigma was, apparently, very great and must be removed at all costs. So some of Bobby's friends, young fellows he had been hanging out with for years, joined the tartan gangs and started beating him up and knocking at our hall-door chanting 'Catholics out!' As you can imagine, it was no easy job to restrain my brother.

Then one day this hag from the UDA came along. She used to go around with young married couples (Protestants, naturally), pointing out the Catholic houses and asking if they liked them. If the answer was yes, their problems were over: the house was available.

So it was that, one unusually sunny afternoon, I was on my way to meet someone when I saw this old witch showing our house to a pair of young newly-weds. I had the distinct feeling that soon we'd be moving out. In fact, one week later we were practically driven out; first a dustbin came crashing through the sitting-room window, spilling garbage all over the carpet; next, every window in the house was smashed with stones; in the end they started shooting at the front door with revolvers.

My Brother Bobby 99

When we came to Twinbrook, in June 1972, we felt like we had reached the Promised Land; for the first time we went to school, to mass, to the youth club with the same friends we used to go around with every day. For folks who had lived in a state of constant siege, this was a dream. Nearly every family in Twinbrook had been forced to leave the place where they had lived before. Some had had to get out so quickly they hadn't time to take a stick of furniture with them; others had taken up residence in houses that were still under construction, but we all helped one another. Marcella, Bobby and myself went round the neighborhood with thermos bottles full of hot tea and milk, to help the families with a lot of children. There was a couple with ten children and the youngest one was mad about Bobby. Every time he saw him he used to throw his arms round his neck and wouldn't let go. Bobby used to say: 'Okay, you can be the fifth baby in our family'. And in fact that's how it was in reality.

But, in 1973, Bobby was arrested, right there in Twinbrook. He was charged with being a full-time republican militant; in substance, in the eyes of the British establishment, this meant that he was a terrorist. During the early months of 1973 he was given a five-year prison sentence for being a 'republican activist'. He spent the next three years behind bars in Long Kesh as a political prisoner. It was there that he learned Gaelic, the ancient language of the Irish people. Later on he would teach it to the other prisoners in the H-Blocks.

Bobby was released from jail in 1976 and he returned to Twinbrook. But in October of the same year he was once again arrested and sentenced to fourteen years, to be served once more in the H-Blocks.

During his six months of freedom in Twinbrook, Bobby seemed much more mature in his way of thinking and behaving. It didn't matter who he was talking to; everyone listened without noticing his age. He made a deep impression on everyone he happened to meet. After he came home,

100 Women's Stories from the North of Ireland

seeing that we had no Green Cross and no Sinn Féin branch, he quickly set up both. He became an active member of the Tenants' Association and he arranged for the black taxis to come as far as Twinbrook from Barrack Street (since public transport at the time was a bad joke). He also established a 'News-sheet' which was distributed all over our neighbourhood, as well as a Sinn Féin bulletin called *Saoirse*.

He contacted a whole lot of people, wealthy and not so wealthy, who were prepared to lend a hand. He went around scrounging for housing, storage space, furniture, cars and all kinds of goods and chattels that might be useful in an experimental neighbourhood like Twinbrook. Bobby's popularity grew so fast that people even used to come to our door asking for him to intervene with the police to try and get private cars to slow down in our streets so the kids would be safe.

I remember the first time the police arrested Bobby, although they couldn't hold him for long. They picked him up along with Marcella and took them both to Fort Monagh. As soon as she heard the news my mother rushed over there and demanded to have her children returned to her: 'You can have the girl back', said the commanding officer, 'but not the boy, because he is refusing to co-operate'. The rain was coming down in buckets, so my mother and Marcella had to wait for four hours standing next to the sentry box. When Bobby was finally released it came out that he had been kept standing in the rain all that time simply because he wouldn't give them his name and address. At home my mother wrapped him up and sat him down by the fire because, as you can well imagine, he was running a temperature. Two hours later there was a knock at the front door. It was some young fellows who needed Bobby's help. Even though my mother begged him not to, he got up and went out with his friends. Commitment, for Bobby, came before any other consideration.

My Brother Bobby 101

The rest of the story is well-known. In the H-Blocks of Long Kesh, having exhausted every other form of protest in trying to get the political status recognised, my brother embarked on the hunger strike that ended with his death. On the fortieth day of his fast, in a by-election for the Fermanagh/South Tyrone constituency, he won a seat at Westminster. But even this wasn't enough for the British government. Even this failed to convince them to budge from their hard-line stance. Bobby was, and would remain, a terrorist and was to be treated as such. He was not a political prisoner but merely a common criminal.

A whole chapter could be devoted to the story of the H-Blocks and to the beatings, the oppression and the humiliation the prisoners were subjected to. Half-way through his sixty-six day hunger strike, Bobby told his mother that if he ever made it back home, he would denounce the brutality of British regime in Long Kesh. But he never did make it back home.

Now, five months after his death, after many of his comrades have dramatically followed his example, I think that Bobby did not die for himself. He did not die alone nor did he die for himself alone. Bobby died so that others might live. As the Autumn that Bobby loved so much begins to fade, this is how I, Bernadette Sands, want to remember my brother.

Taken from the Italian weekly Epoca, *November 7th 1981. Article by Francesco Frigieri. Translation by John Graham.*

18.
My Black Taxi
Kathy Hughes – Belfast (1998)

Áine was one of the most important goddesses of Ireland. A legend tells of how a certain warrior by the name of Étar fell in love with her and died of grief when Áine rejected him. She has survived to the present day as Queen of the Fairies in South Munster. She is said to haunt the hill of Knockainey (to which she gave her name), in County Limerick. The Feast of Áine was celebrated on midsummer's night; the country people would march in procession around the hill, bearing torches to be waved above the heads of their cattle and over the fields to protect them and render them fertile.

***

I live in the New Lodge, a nationalist area in North Belfast. I come from a large family. In the seventies, war and violence devastated our district. My cousin was one of the six people killed one Saturday evening in February 1973, in the streets of the New Lodge. In 1977 my uncle was murdered at his place of work by a Protestant fellow worker. I remember the evening when the loyalists set off a bomb in the McGurk's Pub (December 4th 1971). Fifteen people were killed. I was in the street when I heard the explosion. I was with a friend and we ran to see what had happened. I found myself looking at a terrifying scene: lifeless bodies lying on the ground, the injured calling out for help. It isn't easy to explain what a young girl like myself felt when she was confronted with tragic events like this. They were

My Black Taxi 103

incidents which formed part of my day-to-day life. Every day soldiers and policemen came into my area in order to make a shambles of some dwelling or other. The pretext was always to carry out a house-to-house search or maybe to drag someone I knew away in the middle of the night.

One day the police came to take my brother away. He was sixteen years old. Today he is still in prison and he's due for release in September. Another of my brothers, Danny, has served six years in jail. Prison became a second home for them.

After leaving school, I spent most of the day hanging round the streets with my friends. It was hard for a young girl like me to find work in one of the poorest areas of Belfast. The only chance was a job in the little grocery shop round the corner. It was unthinkable to look for a job in other nationalist areas, because it was the same all over. Working in unionist districts meant running the risk of getting killed. We residents of New Lodge lived from day to day inside the invisible walls that surrounded our neighbourhood. And yet we were very close. We would share the little we had with others who had even less.

In 1973 my mother, my brothers, my sister and myself moved to England, near Blackpool. My father was a sailor and he used to spend long stretches of time away from home, travelling round the world. He would be back for a couple of months and then he'd be off again. We spent three years in England. My mother didn't like living there and neither did we. I remember my first day of school. As soon as they heard I was from Belfast, my school-mates started to avoid me. The teachers themselves were very hard on me. One of them was worse than the others. So, during lunch hour, I left the school and went home. I told my mother I did not want to set foot in the school again. The surprise came when I heard that my brothers and my sister had done the same thing.

Life was hard in that village. Everyone knew we were from Belfast. If something happened, they would come to my

104 *Women's Stories from the North of Ireland*

mother to accuse my brothers. If there was a theft in some shop, then it must have been them. The last straw came when someome smashed the window of the village supermarket and got away with a lot of stuff. They rushed over to my mother enquiring into the whereabouts of five kids who happened to be Irish and were, therefore, potential little criminals. For my mother this was really too much. She just couldn't take it any more. And so back we came to Ireland.

The Belfast that we found when we got back was the same Belfast we had left behind. They were really awful years. Repression and violence were a part of the environment in which I spent the rest of my adolescence.

In 1976 the status of political prisoner was abolished in Long Kesh. Prison struggles and street protests began. The police and the army reacted brutally. They continually carried out house searches, arresting young people the same age as me.

To this very day the most painful memory for me is the death of Bobby Sands in May 1981. That night I was woken up by the sound of dustbin lids being banged on the sidewalk. Bobby Sands was dead and this was the only way to let everyone know. There were clashes with the police until morning came and again the next day. A few days later Francis Hughes died too and after him, in the space of a few months, eight more prisoners. For all of us that was a heart-breaking time. There was nothing we could do to stop that relentless wasting away of young lives.

In 1985 I found a job in Dundonald (East Belfast), in a company called Fisherbody. They manufactured seat belts and airbags for Vauxhall cars. It was my job to assemble the various parts of the belts and stitch them together. I used to work the night shifts along with the other women. 98% of the workers were Protestant. It was a hard time. Sometimes someone would go out to the car park during the lunch break and throw a bucket of paint over my car. I used to find notes at my work station saying: 'Be careful on your way home tonight'.

Those were violent years. A lot of nationalist civilians were killed by the loyalist paramilitary groups. Round about the 12th of July, the most important day of the year in the unionist tradition, they ran up British flags all round the factory and things got very tense. I hung on in that factory as long as I could. Then the whole situation became unbearable. I was forced to leave my job even though the pay was very good. I was a nervous wreck and on the edge of a breakdown.

After some time I applied for a job in the same company, this time in West Belfast, where the workforce was 90% Catholic. I felt much safer in that part of town. We got along with our Protestant co-workers and we never had a problem with them. I stayed in that factory for five more years until they decided to shut it down. We workers were given the choice of being laid off or going back to the East Belfast plant. I felt I just couldn't face up to it. The years I had spent in Dundonald had been such a nightmare that I preferred to lose my job.

Overnight, I found myself unemployed. All I had to live on for several months was the dole money which they paid me twice a month. But I couldn't just hang around the house all day doing nothing. One day I came across the driving licence I had taken out years before. I got this sudden idea of taking driving lessons again. I had always known that driving was almost exclusively a male thing. With all the poverty in our area, owning a car was something that most people, women or men, couldn't afford. But if there was a car in the family, it was usually the man who drove it.

I slowly began to become familiar again with the art of driving. And so I decided that my next job would consist of driving one of those black taxis that cruise around the streets of West and North Belfast. It wasn't going to be easy. First of

106 *Women's Stories from the North of Ireland*

all I had to find a way to buy a second-hand taxi. Besides, this was one of the riskiest jobs you could do in the nationalist areas. In recent years, several taxi drivers had been killed by loyalist paramilitary groups. Anyway, I made up my mind that it was worth giving it a try.

It was the autumn of 1996. I went to talk to Jim Neeson, who represented the West Belfast Taxi Association. I asked him what he thought of the idea and he replied: 'Why not?' I wouldn't be the first. There was already another girl doing the route from Castle Street to Andersonstown. At this point all I had to do was to get cracking. I asked the bank for a loan even though I realised it'd take me a long time to repay the debt plus interest. Then I contacted two mechanics I knew who were leaving for London to find spare parts for their cars. They knew how to get hold of a taxi and so they did. It took me a year to pay all the instalments but in the end I managed with no help from anyone.

The day the taxi arrived from London was a special day for me. I was very happy. I spent six weeks practising, driving around the streets near my house. Then I went back to Jim Neeson. He said I could start work and he gave me a taxi driver's card. The route I would be covering went from the city centre through New Lodge as far as Ardoyne.

The evening before my first day on the job I went to see Joe, a taxi driver. I had known for years. He knew why I wanted to talk to him. It wasn't the prospect of having to work hard that scared me; it was the risk. Joe told me I'd have to be very careful. To tell the truth, at that time, I wasn't all that sure I had made the right choice. I was frightened. In the end, though, I decided I had to go ahead. I started working the week before Christmas 1997. There were lots of people to be carried about and I didn't have the time to think about my fears.

Then came that tragic January of 1998, when the loyalists killed nine Catholics. One of them was a private taxi driver

My Black Taxi 107

from Falls Road. One night he got a call from his assassins; he took them to their destination and then they killed him with a bullet to the head. They dumped his body in the middle of the road and disappeared aboard his taxi.

It was hard to go on working. I never took my eyes off the rear-view mirror and I kept a close watch on all my fares as they got in and out. Driving back and forth along my route I got to know nearly all the people who regularly took my taxi to go from Ardoyne to the city centre and back. So whenever I picked up a stranger I would be worried and keep expecting to see them pull a gun out of nowhere and aim it at me. For hours on end all I did was keep looking around, with one eye on the road and the other on my fares. I'd get home in the evening absolutely worn out, with a splitting headache and my nerves in tatters.

It was the same for my fellow drivers. I could see it in their faces even though they didn't say a word to me. They were all very tense. We had to take a thousand precautions. We always had our two-way radios with us so we could report any suspect movements.

At the end of January 1998, after the string of murders by the loyalists, the situation got so dangerous that I had to wear a bullet-proof vest while I was working. The first time I put it on I felt panicky. It offered only partial protection. What use would it be if they shot me in the head?

That really was the blackest period. I was so scared that I felt like chicking it in. My family and friends kept telling me to change job. But one evening, when I was all alone, I realised I had to go on. If everyone had given up, what would the people in our area do without our service? For fifteen years the black taxis had been driving round the streets of Ardoyne and New Lodge from morning till night, carrying hundreds of passengers every day. All this could not just suddenly stop. And so I decided that, no matter what, I had to go on. They were difficult months. Then hope began

108 *Women's Stories from the North of Ireland*

to dawn among the people that things might change. There were other attempts to assassinate nationalists, but things weren't as bad as they had been in the past. Since that time the situation is less tense and our work is much easier now.

I enjoy my work. I like driving my taxi and meeting lots of people. My mates are always ready to oblige me when I have some trouble with the engine. I like being with them, down at the taxi rank in Castle Street, even though, with our work, we often haven't a minute to exchange a word.

Sometimes I'm asked how I feel compared to all the other women in my area who lead such different lives. I have no family, no children and this is certainly unusual for a woman of my age. Still I don't feel they have something that I haven't. Some of them say they'd like to trade places with me. They have children to bring up and it's really tough. They tell me that I'm lucky to be able to be out of the house for so long, especially during the summer when the weather is fine. And then I can organise my work to suit myself. I work a lot but if I want to take a day off, I can. I don't know if I'll do this work for the rest of my life, but certainly for a few years more.

My mother would love to buy a house in Donegal, to spend the holidays or to get away from Belfast when things get tense again around the 12th of July, on account of the Orangemen's marches. Sooner or later I reckon I'll manage to buy a house in Donegal. A couple of years ago I saw one for sale in a marvellous spot. I was on the dole then, so I couldn't get a mortgage. Nobody bought it for eighteen months. But sadly, after I started working and went to ask about the price, they told me it was gone.

Recorded in Belfast, August 1998

19.
The Money is Never Enough
Christine - Derry (1994)

In Ulster Cailleach Bheara was the name given to the 'old crone', also known as the 'water witch'. She was a spirit of the lake waters and she kept them from drying up. When announcing the approach of a storm, she would take on the form of a crane carrying a bundle of twigs in its beak. Seven times she passed through her youthful womanhood which she spent with seven different husbands. It was Cailleach Bheara who created the mountains; she wore an apron filled with stones until strings would break and all the rocks would tumble down to form gigantic mounds.

***

Christine and Marion live in the nationalist area of Shantallow, in Derry. According to the Northern Ireland Council for Voluntary Action (NICVA) this area has the highest poverty rate in the city. The local newsletter, *Fingerpost*, goes even further and describes it as the most poverty-stricken of the 566 districts in the North of Ireland. Again according to NICVA statistics, 20% of the houses are overcrowded. It is against this background that the dramatic story of these two women is played out.

***

I am thirty years old and I am an unmarried mother. I live in Shantallow with my four children: Gemma (12), Carla (8), Jason (7), and Christina (6).

110 *Women's Stories from the North of Ireland*

Every day I have to face up to a dreadful reality. At times the stress simply wears me out completely. I get £74 social welfare benefits a week. Then there is the £10 from the Enterprise Ulster Workscheme, plus £40 in family benefits. But it's not enough to feed and clothe five people. One sack of coal costs £11.50. We need two sacks a week. Since I can't afford to buy two, the house goes unheated half the time. I've got an electric fire as well but we can't use it very often because it costs too much. The electricity bill comes to £92 every three months. Because the electricity costs so much, I even fiddled the meter. But they found out and now they deduct £10 a week from my welfare cheques.

Although I spend £50 a week on food, sometimes I haven't got the money to buy milk for the kids' breakfast before they go to school. It's a real struggle every week. Every penny goes on bills and expenses. Sometimes, when I go to the supermarket, I get panicky thinking I won't have enough to pay for the stuff I have put in the trolley.

There were times when I had to go to the St. Vincent de Paul's to ask if they could give me a bit of money. It's so humiliating, having to beg. A couple of weeks ago I was so deep in debt that I got up the nerve to go and talk to one of the priests at the Vincent de Paul's. I told him I had no food at all in the house. He gave me some money, but it was only a drop in the bucket. I even asked some of my friends for £5 so's I could scrape together an evening meal for the kids.

A while ago I went to the Department of Social Security asking for a loan. It was a really embarrassing experience. Those people there, the clerks at the DSS I mean, they treat you as if you were taking the money out of their own pockets. They're real off-hand and hoity-toity; they throw all these forms at you one after the other and tell you to fill them in. They couldn't care less about you.

I contacted the Social Welfare people as well. After a bit they sent someone to assess the living conditions in the house and

The Money is Never Enough 111

to calculate how much money the family would need for food. For these people, you're just another 'case' to be dealt with and they examine your whole life through their microscopes.

I went into post-natal depression twice. The social workers were in the house all the time checking up. As an unmarried mother I wasn't even allowed to leave the house. If I did, I'd be accused of neglecting the children and I'd run the risk of having them taken from me. That's the kind of psychological pressure that destroys you from the inside. I've got no one at all to lend me a hand. I end up, like lots of other unmarried mothers, by having to rely on my eldest daughter for help and she's only twelve. So every day I find myself having to load her down with responsibilities that are too much for a little girl of her age.

There's always something going wrong, because the money is never enough. However, there are people who are worse off than me. In my neighbourhood there's kids going round in broken-down shoes and cotton clothes, even in the middle of winter...

Taken from 'Deprivation behind Derry's facelift', An Poblacht/Republican News, April 14th 1994, pp. 8-9

20.
My Husband Has Been Unemployed
for Seventeen Years
Marion McGilloway - Derry (1994)

Fliodhais was a goddess who wandered about the countryside. She ruled over the animal world and embodied the concepts of fertility and the freedom of nature. Her name means 'Mistress of the Deer'. She travelled on a cart drawn by magic deer. She owned a cow which could give enough milk in the course of a single night to nourish three hundred people. Fliodhais regarded all the wild beasts of the countryside as her own. She had a daughter, Fland, a virgin of the lake who lived under water and lured men down to her dwelling place and to their deaths.

***

I live in Shantallow with my husband and our six children. The oldest is seventeen and the youngest is two and a half. My husband Philip has been out of work for seventeen years. There are some part-time jobs going in the commercial centres but they pay very low wages. The only full-time employment to be had is in the security forces (the police or the army); the second requires the sort of qualifications that my husband just hasn't got.

Our eldest son is a fisherman, but all he can get is seasonal work. Our second son is unemployed. He did a two-year stint as an apprentice house painter. Now he can't find anyone who'll give him a job so that he can complete his training. If he doesn't do that, he'll never be able to find steady work. He's in a vicious circle and there's no way out. Our youngest daughter wants to leave school this year and go to work in a

My Husband Has Been Unemployed for Seventeen Years 113

factory. There's not much chance of that on account of the numbers of young people who are out of work in this area. If she can't find work she'll have to go back to school, but my husband and I aren't in a position to finance her studies.

There's a very high percentage of young people living in Shantallow and most of them have no work and no future. Drink and drugs are the most common problems. This is true not only in Derry, but in other areas of Northern Ireland as well. In Shantallow there are no facilities for young people. If they are not offered some kind of hope in the shape of job prospects and social/educational structures, conditions in this area will deteriorate even further and fuel the culture of desperation and criminality.

Shantallow has a population of about 200,000. There's a library, the Housing Executive office, the DSS offices, two post offices and two chemist's shops. There's not one public telephone. No sports centre; the nearest one is the Templemore Sports Complex, on the road to Buncrana, but that's too far away for someone living in my area.

My house is too small for eight people; it's only got three tiny bedrooms. We can't leave it because we wouldn't know where to go. The housing situation in Shantallow is very bad. There are 1,600 people on the waiting list for a house. Since there's no more room, they're even building blocks of flats in what were originally green belts. They've started putting up buildings where families have to live literally on top of one another. The population is being herded into a ghetto. Shantallow is a 'no-man's-land'. It is only recently that they opened the Ardinamoyle playground. This is the only safe place open for hundreds of children – unless you count the streets.

Taken from 'Deprivation behind Derry's facelift', An Poblacht/Republican News, April 14th 1994, pp. 8-9

21.
With Other Women Where the State is Absent
Oonagh Marron - Belfast (1997)

Oonagh was the most beautiful of all the Fairy Queens of Ireland. Her golden tress brushed the ground. She glided over the earth wearing a dress made of a spider's web covered with dew drops. She lived with Finnbheara, the King of the Fairies of Connacht. He betrayed her over and over again with mortal women. And yet this never altered Oonagh's sweet, affectionate character.

***

I am in charge of the Falls Women's Centre. It is located in Falls Road, West Belfast. I have been working there for over ten years.

Falls Road is a nationalist area with a very high unemployment rate. It also has serious problems which are the result of a conflict which has lasted for more than thirty years. It's unbelievable to see how, in such a situation, women manage to organise themselves to help other women. They do it in spite of the innumerable hardships that are part of their own daily lives.

The people who make use of our services come from all over Belfast and its outskirts. Most of them belong to the nationalist working class. Their ages range from eighteen to sixty. Some are extremely poor. They come to us because they haven't enough money to meet their everyday expenses. Others are unmarried mothers who have to rely totally on meager handouts from the Social Welfare. Still others were subjected to sexual violence or have to cope with serious family problems. We try to show these women that they are not alone. The Centre can become a starting point from which they can set out to solve their problems. We refer them on to the specialists: psychotherapists, gynaecologists, lawyers.

Some of the young unmarried mothers we see are still going to school. There are even some, thankfully few, fourteen-year-olds. In addition to medical assistance, we also offer a consulting service. It provides them with advice concerning the social welfare benefits they are entitled to as well as information on training courses they can attend to complete their schooling or to find a job.

Similar centres can be found in other nationalist areas of Belfast, like Poleglass.

Another very active women's centre is located in the unionist Shankill Road. The women who live in unionist areas have to deal with problems of a different kind compared to their opposite numbers. Northern Ireland is a microcosm made up of very dissimilar worlds. Discrimination, arbitrary arrests, repression by the police and the army heavily affect the lives of people living in nationalist areas. Yet they impact hardly at all on the day-to-day life of large portions of the rest of the population.

Take for instance the question of employment. The 1991 census showed that women from Catholic areas are the most likely to be unemployed or to have access only to the most badly-paid, menial jobs. In the case of these women, one may truly speak in terms of a history of poverty handed down from one generation to the next. Today many of them are unemployed just like their mothers, their grandmothers and their great-grandmothers before them. In the case of the male population, the situation is even worse. Therefore one may with justice speak of the 'generations of the unemployed' when referring to the Catholic working class population of Northern Ireland. And yet, as result of the

116 *Women's Stories from the North of Ireland*

crisis in the traditional areas of industry, unemployment has now begun to affect unionist areas as well, with grave repercussions on the job prospects of the women living there.

In 1989 the Women's Support Network was set up. All the women's centres in Belfast and the surrounding area were connected to one another. Since then our centre has constantly collaborated with all the others. The Network organises monthly meetings, where there is an exchange of information regarding the work done by each centre and a discussion of future joint projects. We have a good relationship, both professional and personal, with the women working in the centres located in unionist areas. This doesn't mean we don't have our problems. When people with different backgrounds find themselves working together there will always be difficulties arising from their different ways of viewing the same reality.

I don't think anybody in Northern Ireland can consider themselves to be neutral. We share the same history: a history of domination and colonialism which to this very day weighs heavily on our daily existence. The life experience of each one of us is affected by our different ways of relating ourselves to this history of domination. As a result, my political ideas are quite different to those of the women who work in unionist areas. Within the Network, we have decided to recognise that these differences do exist. The Network's charter states that we are 'a united voice, the voice of women who claim the right to be different' and who respect 'the fact that others are different'. None of us is expected to think in the same way with respect to the problems of women's education, poverty or the lack of job opportunities for women. The important thing is to find a common basis upon which to build. This is by no means easy but it is only by respecting this diversity that the Network can continue to operate. If we were to pretend that these differences did not exist we would be unable to do anything constructive.

When I speak of a "common ground" existing between them and us, I mean that, working together, we try to identify

With Other Women Where State is Absent 117

those areas relating to the female condition in which, even in the unionist community, the state is absent. It must, however, be borne in mind that unionist women have a quite different relationship vis-à-vis the state. For years the nationalist community was simply ignored by the state. You need only pass through some of the nationalist areas to realise how seriously degraded they are, how they lack even the most basic social structures and how the whole territory is militarized to a degree that has no parallel anywhere in Europe. In order to survive, the nationalist community was compelled to pool its resources and become self-organized, in order to deal with day-to-day problems for which the state had not the slightest intention of assuming responsibility.

Things were very different for the women of the unionist community. From the very outset Northern Ireland was conceived of as being 'a Protestant state for a Protestant people'. As a result of this, only the members of the unionist community have traditionally had access to power within the structures of the state. Until now the economy, local government and the main political and social institutions have been firmly in the grip of the unionists. Unionist citizens were always able to rely on state institutions and local politicians for the solution of their problems. Yet the unionist community is at present experiencing a phase of great uncertainty with respect to a state which, in the past, had always backed them up. They view the new political developments as a gradual eroding of the special relationship with London which they have always enjoyed. Many are apprehensive of the changes taking place because they are worried about losing the privileges which up till now they have always been granted.

As I already said, nowadays it is not always easy to find work even for those who live in unionist areas. This is particularly true in the case of the unskilled workers. It is the unionist working class that has been most seriously affected. This explains why, in these areas, the feeling of having been

118 Women's Stories from the North of Ireland

betrayed by London is stronger. There has been a progressive loss of trust in local politicians. They are considered to be less and less capable of finding solutions to the most pressing social problems of the community. Those politicians have now become even more conservative. Fearful of losing power, they oppose community projects in the most deprived areas.

The example of Shankill Women's Centre is a case in point. The Belfast City Council has just cut off the centre's funding. The women in the centre feel that the unionist institutions such as the Orange Order and the die-hard unionists have done little or nothing to solve the problems concerning the female world. On the contrary, these women want to work in favour of women in areas in which the institutions have always been absent.

This is the context within which the collaboration with the women of the nationalist community has borne fruit. As they are just now beginning to organise themselves they stand to learn a great deal from our long experience in the area of self-help. We, in turn, can derive new ideas and fresh impetus from their different experiences. This will help us to operate more effectively. Today we can work together in joint schemes. We can pressure the state to deal more seriously than it has done in the past with the problems of women of both communities. This shows how false the stereotyped image of the reality of Northern Ireland is. The North is usually depicted as a land where division and hatred have been literally bred into the population. In actual fact there are many people of diverse cultural identities who have been working together for years to solve their common problems and to build a new society. The Network is a clear proof of this.

Recorded in Belfast, August 1997

Biographical Note

Sivia Calamati is both a journalist and a writer. Since 1982 she has concerned herself with the Irish question.

After taking her degree in Philosophy, she spent the years from 1985 to 1986 furthering her studies and carrying out research at the University College Dublin on behalf of the University of Venice.

She has lived in Dublin and Belfast for lengthy periods of time. From 1990 until 1995 she covered Northern Ireland for the Italian weekly *Avvenimenti.*

Since 1995, she has been working as a free-lance journalist for various radio/television stations, both Italian and foreign.

Together with Bjørn Cato Funnemark (Norwegian Helsinki Committee for Human Rights) and Richard Harvey (New York) she is the author of *Irlanda del Nord. Una colonia in Europa* (Edizioni Associate, Rome, 1997).

She has translated into Italian *One day in my life* by Bobby Sands (*Un giorno della mia vita.* Feltrinelli, Rome, 1996) and *Renewing the Irish Church* by father Joe McVeigh (*Guerra e liberazione in Irlanda. La Chiesa del conflitto.* Edizioni della Battaglia, Palermo, 1998).